Forty Days of
Fasting & Prayer
in the Biblical Context

A Kingdom Message for Believers & Unbelievers

Clifford N. Opurum

Trafford rev. 09/13/2016

Trafford
PUBLISHING® www.trafford.com
North America & international
toll-free: 1 888 232 4444 (USA & Canada)
fax: 812 355 4082

DEDICATION

Dedicated to my Lord and Savior, my Redeemer, the KING of Kings and the LORD of Lords

ACKNOWLEDGEMENTS

First and foremost, I must acknowledge and thank my Creator and the Almighty God for His grace and for granting me His divine wisdom and inspiration which I so much needed to write this and my other books. I am equally indebted to my dear parents, the late Mr. & Mrs. Thomas and Juliana Opurum, who, by the grace of God, brought me into this world and taught me the values of a True Believer. Those values are what have helped me to deal with the issues and realities of life, while at the same time, drawing me closer and closer each day to my Creator and Redeemer. I couldn't have asked for better parents.

Indeed, and without reservations, I feel very blessed and grateful to God for giving me the best woman any man can think of as a wife and life partner, my Blessing (Ngo). Together with my dearly beloved children, my Precious Promises of God, they represent priceless gifts of God to me, and something more than any man can ask for a family. They were very much instrumental in the efforts that brought this book to fruition. Their moral supports and their constructive criticisms of the drafts of the manuscripts are without measure.

My special gratitude goes to the Presiding Prelate of the New Covenant Christian Ministries Worldwide, His Grace, Archbishop Dr. Joseph A. Alexander who graciously read the manuscript. As a spiritual leader and mentor, his teachings on the Scriptures were instrumental and motivational to completing this book, and I thank God for him and all that he is doing in bringing the Kingdom of God to the spheres of humanity.

Finally, I give glory to God for my dear siblings who, though are not physically with me on a daily basis due to the geographical gap between us, have always prayed for me and encouraged me in all my endeavors. May God richly bless each and every one of them, and grant them the desires of their hearts.

PREFACE

This book is based on my spiritual experiences and observations within Christ-centered environment in my daily walk with my Creator King, God during the October –November 2011 Forty Days of Fasting and Prayers at the New Covenant Christian Ministries (NCCM) in New York City. It is written under the inspiration of the Holy Ghost, and the gift of divine wisdom, knowledge and understanding received from God as I trusted and obeyed Him.

During that fasting season, and as I walked closer and closer to God Almighty day after day, I felt anointed and inspired, and thus developed a sense of deeper spiritual maturity in God's divine agenda. This goes to support and truly confirm God's instruction to us that if we draw near to Him, He will draw near to us. Indeed, my experience during those Holy Ghost-filled forty days and forty nights could be likened to the experiences of the Apostles in the Upper Room on the day of The Pentecost. In a nut-shell, and in fact, I thought of The Rapture at the end of that fasting and prayer season. It's worth every moment of it, and as I felt saturated with divine anointing and moving in the power of the Holy Ghost.

On October 2, 2011, the Presiding Prelate of the New Covenant Christian Ministries Worldwide (NCCM), His Grace, Archbishop Dr. Joseph A. Alexander proclaimed a Forty-Day Fasting and Prayer program for the first time in the twenty-nine-year history of the Ministries (as of that date). This move was prompted most importantly by the growing need for the believers to have a closer relationship with God as the world continued to immerse deeper and deeper into abominations and immoralities. It was also meant to spiritually enable the believers in the Ministries to intercede for the sick and the weak, the lost, the hopeless, the unbelieving souls and the hard-hearted as a part of the True Discipleship mandate.

The world we live in today is full of "hustle and bustle" or the so called "rat race" to nowhere but to "the bottom". This is more so, if you live in a metropolitan area such as the New York Metropolitan Region where I reside and where everybody is always in a rush; always running and rarely walking. It has become a place where no one seems to have any time to "stop and smell the roses", and to observe, reflect and enjoy God's marvelous creation. It has become a place where everyone seems to be on the highway instead of the byways or better still, pulling into the driveway. But in the mist of all these, it is imperative that we find time for a quiet moment within our hearts to commune with our heavenly father, and to have a dialogue with Him in our individual "war rooms".

One thing each and every one of us must understand is that when it is all said and done, and as the smoke clears and the ashes settle, it is what we have done for God and our relationship with Him that really matters. It is not how many mansions we own, how many jumbo jets we have acquired, nor the fleet of Rose Royce we have that matters. Indeed, it is not how high we climbed on the corporate ladder or the level of political office, nor is it how many billions or trillions of dollars we have accumulated that matters.

We must strive to labor diligently in God's vineyard and remain steadfast while doing so in order to ensure that our names are indelibly written in the Lambs Book of Life (the listing of Who is Who in the Kingdom of the Most High God, and which cannot be re-cycled). Let us not be found wanting when the trumpet sounds and the final roll call is made. We no doubt can stand a better chance of doing so only by fasting and praying without ceasing. This book will immensely help you, and encourage you in positioning yourself for a place in the Kingdom of God.

As you read through the pages of this book and you have not yet surrendered your life totally to Jesus, I implore you to do so immediately and be reconciled to God today. I graciously urge you not to procrastinate on this imperative matter for indeed, tomorrow may be too late; behold, this is the day of salvation.

Deacon Dr. Clifford N. Opurum, PhD, MCIT

Contents

CHAPTER 1

Introduction

Jesus said to his disciples: *"Howbeit, this kind goeth not out but by prayer and fasting" (Matt 17:21)*. Throughout the Scriptures, and indeed the history of humanity, true servants of God have fasted and prayed as they faced circumstances that were above and beyond human comprehension and capability. They understood the importance of fasting and prayer as they become over-whelmed with trials and tribulations, and with other unimaginable afflictions, including spiritual attacks of this secular world. Consider, for instance, the case of King Jehoshaphat in II Chronicles 20, and his encounter with the Ammonites, the Moabites and the children of Mount Seir as we shall read later in Chapter 2.

"Howbeit, this kind goeth not out but by prayer and fasting" (Matt 17:21)

Recall the case of Hannah, one of the two wives of Elkanah of Ramathaim-zophim, in the Book of 1 Samuel Chapter 1 as she fasted, prayed, and cried unto the Lord, with perseverance and steadfastness in her desperate need for a child (who shall later be named Samuel, the covenant child). Fasting is a spiritual discipline of the flesh, while prayer is the spiritual act of faith through which we communicate with God. Together, they represent the greatest weapon we can use to confront and defeat the common enemy, Satan. We fast and pray because there is a cause. Also, since manifestation is the spiritual brain child of expectation,

We fast and pray because there is a cause. when we fast and pray we must do so in faith, and come with the spirit of expectation in order for us to experience any form of manifestation.

Think also of the first thing Jesus did immediately after His baptism as He was led into the wilderness by the Spirit, and what He was doing in the Garden of Gethsemane as His hour approached during that historical period. Did He not go to a quiet corner in that garden, and away from His disciples to fast and pray before the arrival of the Roman soldiers that night?

The biography of Jesus in the New Testament shows that it was only after He returned from the forty days of fasting and prayer that He began His healing ministry here on earth. There is no record in the Scriptures of Jesus ever performing any healing miracle, prior to that event. For the Believer, fasting and prayer represent the most powerful tool available to combat and ward-off the common enemy and the adversary, Satan and all its agents and co-conspirators. Together, fasting and prayer aligns us with God's plan, priority and purpose.

As we fast and pray, we tend to feel that inner spiritual uplifting and satisfaction as we enjoy the privilege of drawing nearer and nearer to our Heavenly Father and Creator. It makes us feel His very presence, and we know that in His presence that there is fullness of joy and His Joy gives us strength. Remember that God has promised us that if we draw near to Him, He will draw near to us, and the believer understands that His words are yeah and amen.

Fasting and prayer enables us to have a closer and more personal relationship with God. Personally, fasting and praying gives the same indescribable spiritual feeling I experienced immediately after my water baptism by immersion several years ago as I emerged out of that water as a new creation, having buried the "old things" underneath the water as with Christ and then rose again anew. In Chapter 6 verse 4 of his letter to the Romans, the Apostle Paul writes *"Therefore we are buried with him by baptism into death: that as Christ was raised up from the dead by the glory of the Father, even so we also shall walk in newness of life"*.

Fasting and prayer, together, provides the confidence and strength that the believer needs to overcome the trials and tribulations that we face day after day. Particularly, it enables us to resist the devil, and which makes him to flee from us. For spiritual growth and maturity, it is imperative therefore, that we fast and pray. When we fail to fast and pray, we make ourselves vulnerable to the attacks of the enemy who is always wondering as a roaring lion looking for who to devour.

The Collins English Dictionary defines a fast as the act of abstaining from eating all or certain foods or meals, (especially, as a religious observance). Similarly, it defines prayer as a personal communication or petition addressed to a deity, especially in the form of supplication, adoration, praise, contribution or thanksgiving, or any other form of spiritual communion with a deity. Here, we see prayer as the key with which we get into God's holy presence in order to commune with Him, and to experience signs and wonders as we make our requests known to Him, while also equipping ourselves to withstand the forces of darkness, and principalities and powers.

On October 2, 2011, the Presiding Prelate of the New Covenant Christian Dominion Ministries Worldwide (NCCDM), His Grace, Archbishop Dr. Joseph A. Alexander proclaimed a Forty-Day Fasting, Prayer and Consecration for the first time in the twenty-nine-year history of the Ministries. This move was prompted most importantly by the growing need for the believers to draw nearer to God and to have a closer relationship with Him as the world continued to immerse deeper and deeper into abominations and immoralities, even beyond the immoral behaviors of the days of Sodom and Gomorrah in the days of Abraham. (Bible scholars and other believers will recall that Abraham persevered in his intercessory negotiation with God on behalf of the people of Sodom and Gomorrah to see if they could identify at least five individuals whose hearts were right with God, but to no avail. It was at that point that the negotiation ended and God had to do what is right with Him. As of this work, laws have been passed in several nations and regions of the world stating that a man can marry another man and a woman another woman, and granting them the same legal rights as the one granted to couples in traditional holy matrimony. It was for this same reason that God utterly destroyed Sodom and Gomorrah. The fact that we have so much more intercessors today than was the case in the days of Sodom and Gomorrah is the reason why God has continued to grant us His grace and ceaselessly sparing us in this immoral world wherein we dwell.)

That solemn assembly was also meant to spiritually enable the believers in the Ministries to intercede for the sick and the weak, the lost, the hopeless, the unbelieving souls and the hard-hearted, the A'habs and Jezebels, and all lovers of evil as a part of the true discipleship mandate[1]. It has been said that prayer is the key that opens locked doors, but here we understand and believe that fasting and prayer, together, represent the arsenal the believer needs to spiritually pull down the enemy strong holds, breaking every chain and setting the captives free.

This book is written under the inspiration of the Holy Ghost, and the gift of divine knowledge, wisdom and understanding received from God as the author trusted and obeyed Him. It is based on the author's spiritual experiences and observations within Christ-centered environment in his daily walk with our Creator King and Redeemer during the October – November 2011 and the October-December 2012, respective Forty Days of Fasting, and Prayers seasons at the New Covenant Christian Dominion Ministries (NCCDM) in New York City, New York, U.S.A. It is written for both the believers and the unbelievers. Indeed, it is meant for everyone including the faithful and the faithless, the hopeful and the hopeless, the broken-hearted, and to all who want to have a closer, quiet, and intimate relationship with our Creator, the Almighty God.

It is the duty of every believer to pray every day and to fast periodically as often as possible so as to withstand temptations and over-come every plan of the enemy. Let's make it a routine to fast and pray. Christians have been instructed by Jesus to watch and pray until He returns on earth from His Father, and that no one, no not even Himself knows neither the day nor the hour when that shall happen. Fasting and prayer will keep us spiritually alert, and help us not to miss the sounding of the trumpet and the marching of the Saints on that day as the Christ returns.

Remember the parable of the ten virgins as told by Jesus in Matt. 25$^{:1-13}$. In the last four verses of that Scripture, vv.10-13, we read of the response that Jesus (the Bridegroom) gave to the foolish virgins who returned late from their oil shopping trip because they did not take any oil with them for their lamps. Hence, they weren't ready for the Bridegroom at the unpredictable time of His return. The Scripture tells us that while these foolish virgins were gone for the oil, the Bridegroom arrived, and the door was locked, and when they knocked desperately for the door to be opened and as they said: *"Lord, Lord open for us"*, the Lord responded and said to them that He knew them not. In v.13, Jesus says to us: *"Watch therefore, for ye know neither the day nor the hour wherein the Son of man cometh"*. Indeed, men ought to watch and pray without ceasing as the Scripture teaches us. Jesus tells us in His Gospel according to Saint John Chapter 16[:33B], *"In the world ye shall have tribulation: but be of good cheer; I have overcome the world"*.

We should therefore not relent in our efforts in remaining steadfast unto our faith, while being mindful of the devices of the enemy who comes but to steal, to kill and to destroy. We can be able to do this only by fasting and prayer, while looking up to Jesus, who is the Author and Finisher of our faith. We must, therefore, watch and pray without ceasing, since the adversary comes just as a thief.

This book has been ideally organized in a way to enable the readers develop some spiritual thoughts, and to gain some insights as they progress through the pages of the text. In this chapter, an overview of fasting and prayer, as well as the motivational factor that inspired the author to write this book are featured.

Chapter 2: Why Fast and Pray for Forty Days: The Biblical Significance, features the significance of fasting and prayers as evidenced throughout the Scripture and presents some documented examples and evidences. The subject of Chapter 3 is The Body of Christ and True Discipleship. In Chapter 4 we look at the Spiritual, Physical and Socioeconomic Benefits of Fasting and Praying. The Daily Activities and Experiences during the Forty Days of fasting and prayers programs in October – November 2011, and in October-December 2012, respectively, are also featured in that chapter.

Chapter 5 focuses on Covenanting with God and Walking in The Spirit. The connection between Fasting and Biblical Counseling is examined in Chapter 6. Chapter 7 considers why we should let go and let God take-over our circumstances and situations as true believers, and then reviews the power of forgiveness and the consequences of unforgiveness. In Chapter 8 we reflect on What We Have Learned, and in the last chapter, Chapter 9, we read about how we must live our lives Moving Forward.

CHAPTER 2

Why Fast and Pray For Forty Days: The Biblical Significance

In the Bible, the number 'forty" is very significant. First and foremost, our Lord and Savior Jesus Christ fasted for forty days and forty nights before He was led into the wilderness to be tempted by the devil. Similarly, Moses the Law Giver and Prophet of God fasted for forty days and forty nights in his desperate desire to seek the face of the Lord and to hear from Him (Exodus 34:28). In fact, the Scripture tells us that Moses did neither drink water nor ate any bread (food) for those forty days and forty nights as he communed with God face to face on Mount Sinai.

In part B of that same Scripture (Exodus 34:28), the Bible says: *"And he (Moses) wrote upon the tables the words of the covenant, the Ten Commandments"*. Before this time, God had already instructed Moses in Exodus

34$^{:27}$ saying: *"....Write thou these words: for after the tenor of these words I have made a covenant with thee and with Israel"*. In fact, as we read through the entire Book of Exodus, we understand that it was indeed due to the intimate relationship Moses established with God through fasting and prayers that He (God) promised and drove away all the "ites" and "sites" out of the way to the promised land, Canaan, in order for His people, the Israelites to enter and inherit the land. (For the sake of those who are not very familiar with this portion of the Scripture), these "ites" and "sites" include the Amorites, Canaanites, Hittites, Perizzites, Hivites, Amelekites, the Jebusites (and later on, the Philistines). These were very powerful groups of people and the Israelites could not have defeated any of these if God was not on their side in each of the encounters.

In the Epistle of Paul the Apostle to the Ephesian Church as in Ephesians 1$^{:18}$, the Scripture states as follows: *"The eyes of your understanding being enlightened; that ye may know what is the hope of his calling, and what is the riches of the glory of his inheritance in the saints"*. Moses was very desirous of knowing the hope of God's calling, so as to walk, and work according to his purpose, plan and priority. He knew that for him to have an intimate relationship with God, and to hear directly from Him, requires that he sanctify and consecrate himself, and live an unpolluted, unadulterated, worthy life.

In the days of Noah, God caused the earth to be flooded for forty days, and forty nights. Indeed, the great journey with our creator is a wonderful experience as we walk in faith, and in obedience. We walk with God not in ignorance, but with positive attitude and optimism, while looking unto Jesus the Author and Finisher of our faith in every step of the way in our journey with Him. In Joel 2:12-13, God spoke to us through His prophet, Prophet Joel, and said: "Therefore also now saith the Lord, turn ye even to me with all your heart, and with fasting, and with weeping, and with mourning; And rend your heart, and not your garments, and turn unto the Lord your God; for He is gracious and merciful, slow to anger, and of great kindness, and repenteth Him of the evil".

The purpose of fasting is to spiritually clear our minds and body and thereby reconcile our spirit, soul and body. Because these three are often in a battle, it becomes imperative for us to often fast and pray so as to make room for reconciliation. Together, fasting and prayer is a spiritual thing and it requires self-discipline of the soul and body and of course, with the help of the Holy Spirit.

The purpose of fasting is to spiritually clear our minds and body and thereby reconcile our spirit, soul and body.

Fasting helps to keep us focused by enabling us to resist the lust of the flesh, and as we walk in the Spirit. As Apostle Paul wrote in his letter to the Church in Rome (Romans 13:14): "But put ye on the Lord Jesus Christ, and make no provision for the flesh to fulfill the lust thereof", we must not invite any element of corruption into our lives.

11

When we fast and pray in spirit and in truth, we are indeed exchanging the burden of heaviness we carry daily with the garment of praise. It means, as God has said in Isaiah 60:3, giving up ashes for beauty, and receiving the oil of joy for mourning. Fasting helps us to get rid of the greatest enemy of man that is constantly threatening us; fear, which our common enemy and the adversary, the devil uses as its most powerful tool and weapon to try to confuse, distract, divide, demean, distort, disorganize, disgrace, belittle, humiliate, demoralize, and then weaken us.

When we fast and pray in spirit and in truth, we are indeed exchanging the burden of heaviness we carry daily with the garment of praise.

It prepares and positions us to spiritually receive the full benefits of the blessings of the Lord, as we honor Him. Again as we do so, we are indeed consecrating ourselves to move to a higher spiritual level.

From the believer's perspective, we may consider the following qualitative formula, which we may refer to as the **True Believer's Model** for fasting and prayer, and with this model we can say that: $[F+(P.Pr)]^2 = Pw$ to C & G,

Where: F = Fasting;
P = Prayer;
Pr = Praise;
Pw = Power;
C = Conquer; and
G = Govern.

In other words, we can simply say that when we have a divine and spiritual package of fasting and prayer, and then seal it with the highest level of praise, we are strategically positioning ourselves spiritually to conquer the common enemy, Satan and thereafter exercise our rightful authorities to govern, rule, and take dominion on the earth as the authentic representatives of the Most High God, Jehovah, here on planet earth.

We must not forget that God abides in the praises of His people, and that praises are an important component of fasting and prayers. We also know that as praises go up, blessings come down. Fasting and prayer can bring generational or ancestral curse to an end, and fasting reminds us that the body is subject to the Spirit. We need to seek the grace to take dominion and be moved to think and act like God.

Forty days is very symbolic in the practice of fasting and praying. As has been hinted earlier in Chapter 1, our Lord and Savior Jesus Christ taught us to do so by living by example, as He was led by the Spirit into the wilderness immediately after His baptism by John The Baptist in River Jordan, and fasted for forty days and forty nights before He was tempted by the devil. The Scripture in the Gospel of Jesus Christ according to Saint Matthew, Chapter 4[1-11], narrates Jesus' encounter with the devil just after He ended His fasting session in the wilderness. Reading from vs.1 through v.11 of Matt. 4, the Scripture says *"Then was Jesus led up of the Spirit into the wilderness to be tempted by the devil. And* *when he had fasted for forty days and forty nights, he was afterward an hungered. And when the tempter came to him, he said, If thou be the Son of God, command that these stones be made bread. But he answered and said, It is written, **Man shall not live by bread alone, but by every word that proceedeth out of the mouth of God**.*

*Then the devil taketh him up into the holy city, and sitteth him on the pinnacle of the temple, and saith unto him, If thou be the Son of God, cast thyself down: for it is written, He shall give his angels charge concerning thee: and in their hands they shall bear thee up, lest at any time thou dash thy foot against a stone. Jesus said unto him, It is written again, **Thou shall not tempt the Lord thy God**. Again, the devil taketh him up into an exceeding high mountain, and showeth him all the kingdoms of the world, and the glory of them; And saith unto him, All these things will I give thee, if thou wilt fall down and worship me. Then saith Jesus unto him, Get thee hence, Satan: for it is written, **Thou shall worship the Lord thy God, and Him only shall thou serve**. Then the devil leaveth him, and, behold, angels came and ministered unto him".*

In a very simple language, the phrase, "get thee hence, Satan" means get thee behind me, Satan, as other versions of the Bible phrased it, or as the carnally-minded will put it: "Get out of my face you silly thing". Undoubtedly, it takes the anointing of God for anyone to be able to command Satan in this manner and succeed in getting rid of him.

The Gospel according to Saint Luke in Chap. 4, and v.13 also tells us that *"when the devil had ended all the temptation, he departed from Him for a season"*. Notice that the Scripture did not tell us that the devil departed from Him indefinitely and never to return to Him. Rather, what we are told is that the devil *"departed from Him for a season"*. What does this then mean to each and every one of us? It means that our indulgence in the act and practice of fasting and prayer must be systematic, consistent, and with perseverance. We must endeavor to remain steadfast in the Lord.

We must therefore continue to pray without ceasing, so as to remain prepared and well equipped; always ready to ward-off the enemy whenever he comes to temp, deceive, confuse, ridicule, embarrass, and tries to humiliate and shame us. The Scripture tells us that men ought to pray without ceasing. Our Lord and Savior is the greatest teacher we can ever learn from, and He lived by examples for He never ceased to pray. He is indeed The Rabbi (The Master Teacher).

In addition to many other countless instances in the Scripture, Saint Luke, in his account of the Gospel of Jesus Christ, recorded in Luke 6:12 regarding the habitual prayer life of the Master Teacher (Jesus) and states as follows: *"Now it came to pass in those days that (Jesus) went out to the mountain to pray, and continued all night in prayer to God"*. When we think of praying without ceasing, we must also not forget that he, Satan is in enmity with God and if that is the case, what then makes us think that he will be our best friend, since we are the children of his enemy, the Almighty God, and our Creator King. We must not let the enemy take us unawares by not watching and praying without ceasing, and by not putting on the whole armor of God, which includes the Sword of the Spirit (the Word of God), the Breastplate of Righteousness, and the Helmet of Salvation, among others.

Obviously, Jesus was able to counter every trick and strategy the devil tried to use to humiliate Him during this encounter because He divinely prepared and readied Himself by equipping Himself with the power of fasting and prayer over the forty days and forty nights of fasting and prayer in the wilderness. Indeed, our Lord Jesus had the pre-knowledge of what challenges he was going to face as He was led into the wilderness by the Spirit. (Notice the uppercase used in the word "Spirit" in this case which signifies the Holy Spirit as against evil spirit.)

In Matt. 17, and regarding the healing of the Demoniac Son, who was referred to as the lunatic (as the disease that afflicted him took-over his identity), in v.21 of that Scripture, Jesus said to His disciples, who were unable to heal this demon- possessed young man when he was presented to them while Jesus was not with them, *"Howbeit, this kind goeth not out but by prayer and fasting"*. In other words, Jesus made it clear to His disciples that by themselves, they have limitations on what they can do, even with prayers alone, and that for some kinds of miraculous works, such as the one they were unable to do by prayer alone, that the joint power of fasting and prayer is imperative.

For those who are not familiar with this extra-ordinary healing story told in Matt. 17:14-21, the Scripture says as follows, and beginning from v.14: *"And when they were come to the multitude, there came to him a certain man, kneeling down to him, and saying, Lord, have mercy on my son: for he is a lunatic, and sure vexed: for ofttimes he falleth into the fire, and oft into the water. And **I brought him to your disciples, and they could not cure him.** Then Jesus answered and said, O faithless and perverse generation, how long shall I be with you? How long shall I suffer you? Bring him hither to me. And Jesus rebuked the devil; and he departed out of him: and the child was cured in that very hour. **Then came the disciples to Jesus apart, and said, Why could we not cast him out? And Jesus said unto them, because of your unbelief**: for verily a say unto you, except, if you have faith as a grain of mustard seed, you shall say unto the mountain, Remove hence to your place; and it shall remove; and nothing shall be impossible unto you. **Howbeit this kind goeth not out but by prayer and fasting"**.*

Fasting could be likened to some track-and-field athletic race in which there are various levels based on the distance to be covered: 100 yards, 220, 440, relay, and ultimately, the marathon, and the distance covered in the race has some bearing on the prize awarded to the athlete at the finish line. There are various levels of fast depending on their lengths and circumstances. The Holy Bible documents three particular types of fast:

- **Absolute or Extreme Fast**
- **Normal Fast, and**
- **Partial Fast.**

The first type of fast, absolute or extreme fast, is what is also known as "dry fast", and in which the observer goes without eating any food or drinking any type of fluid throughout the period of the fast, prayers, praises and supplication. The most noted example of this type of fast is that of Jesus as he was led by the Spirit into the wilderness after His baptism when He fasted for forty days and forty nights. This is the extreme case, and the most powerful type of fast that has ever been practiced among matured believers. However, this type of fast should not be observed for a long period of time since neither food nor drink shall be consumed during the entire fasting period.

Those who engage in this type of fast must be very cautious while engaging in it, and of course, with faith. Should you start to feel dehydrated at any point as you progress in this type of fast, then you must try to drink some juice to hydrate your body and at the same time supply some of the energy that your physical body may require in order to continue to work together with your spirit and soul. Otherwise you may reach that point where the spirit will be willing but the body becomes weak, and you may find yourself ending the fast abruptly, and in disagreement with your original plan and expectations. This is the type of Fast Jesus observed after His baptism, and as He was led into the wilderness by the Holy Spirit before He was tempted by the devil.

The second type of fast is what is known as normal fast, and in which case the participants will not eat any food nor drink any fluid, other than water, for a specified number of days. Again, due to the physical challenges associated with this type of fast, as the body tries to adjust to this sudden and "new" dietary schedule, the length of time for this type of fast should not be too long. During this twelve hour period, the participant(s) will intermittently study the Word of God, sing praises, pray and meditate as they enter into serious dialogue with God; drawing nearer and nearer to God and developing more intimate relationship with Him. Cumulatively, the time spent in each day for studying the Word of God and praying should be at least two and a half (2.5) hours, which is equal to the tithe or approximately ten (10) percent of twenty (24) hours.

The last type of fast is referred to as partial fast and it goes according to its name. This type of fast is also called the "Daniel's Fast", relating to Daniel and his three Hebrew companions' (Shadrack, Meshach, and Abednego) refusal to eat any meat and any sweet thing, or drink any wine from the table of King Nebuchadnezzar at the beginning of their captivity in Babylon. They only requested to be given vegetables and water throughout the period. He (Daniel) later, and as he grieved over the condition of Israel (in Daniel Chapter 10), embarked on another twenty-one day partial fast in which he ate no sweet and no meat, and drank no wine and as he focused on prayer throughout the period of the fast.

Typically, observers of this type of fast will consume neither food nor any drink from sunrise until sunset, or more specifically, from 6:00 a.m. to 6:00 p.m., while intermittently, studying, praying and praising God and meditating on the Word of God with the motive if drawing nearer and having a more intimate relationship with Him. As in the case of the first two types of fast, the participants must endeavor to devote at least ten (10) percent of the time for studying the Word of God, praying, and meditating. Ideally, this type of fast is for those who are not able to withstand the daring demands of the absolute (extreme) fast and normal fast, which could be strenuous, particularly for the young believers.

At the end of the twelve hour period, the observers of this second type of fast may eat and drink to end the day's fasting. However, the food to be consumed in this case is basically fruits and vegetables and water is the only fluid to be drunk. In the case of a corporate fast, it is customary that the participants gather in the house of worship at the end of the day's fasting for a corporate prayer service based on the selected Scripture(s) for the day.

Besides the aforementioned types of fast, there are other types of fast according to the physical and spiritual capabilities of the observers. In some instances, those who observe this type of fast may endeavor to skip at least one meal a day during the period, and they may also drink water or fruit juice at their own discretion, depending on their capabilities, and as long as they are finding some quiet time to draw nearer to God and get to know Him more intimately.

Overall, there is no set rule as to the length of time with respect to fasting, nor is there any set formula for the type of fast that is suitable for anyone. Rather, depending on how individuals feel, and based on the given circumstances that represent the cause for them to make the decision to proclaim a fast, they will determine the type of fast that is suitable for them. Again, try not to go for the type of fast that you are not yet spiritually and physically sound to undertake, or go for a very lengthy period if you are just starting to fast for the first time. You may start with even a half a day fast and gradually get to the extreme type of fast or "dry fast".

Nevertheless, it requires a great deal of zeal and desire for God, and steadfastness, perseverance, faithfulness and obedience to Him to be able to achieve this. All in all, you must ask the Holy Spirit to take absolute control, and to grant you the enablement to be able to do so. In all your efforts, always remember what the Scripture tells us in Philippians 4[:13]: *"I can do all things through Christ who strengthens me"*.

Now, let us consider the case of young King Jehoshaphat in II Chronicles 20, and his encounter with the Ammonites, the Moabites and the children of Mount Seir, and how that story ended. We must bear in mind that King Jehoshaphat was only thirty-five years old when he began to reign over Judah, and reigned in Jerusalem for twenty-five years. The Bible also tells us that he never departed from doing what is right in the sight of God as his father, Asa did.

As the Scripture tells us, King Jehoshaphat *"feared and set himself to seek the Lord and proclaimed a fast throughout all Judah"* (v. 3), as he saw the eminent calamity that was to befall his people. The scripture tells us in v.4 that *"Judah gathered themselves, together to ask help from the LORD"*. In v.14, we were told that upon Jahaziel the son of Zecharaiah, a Levite came the Spirit of the LORD in the mist of the congregation, as He (God) released His prophecy through him and prophesied in vv.15B and 17 saying: *"Be not afraid nor dismayed by reason of this great multitude; for the battle is not yours, but God's". Ye shall not need to fight in this battle; set yourselves, stand ye still, and see the salvation of the LORD with you, O Judah and Jerusalem; fear not nor be dismayed; tomorrow go out against them; for the LORD will be with you"*.

In v.20B of II Chronicles 20, King Jehoshaphat called the attention of his people to God's prophesy regarding their situation and said: *Hear me O Judah and ye inhabitants of Jerusalem; Believe in the LORD your God, so shall ye be established; believe his prophets, so shall ye prosper"*. The Scripture further tells us in v.22 that **as they started to sing and to praise, the LORD set ambushments against the children of Ammon, Moab and Mount Seir, which were come against Judah; and they were smitten**. In this case, the Lord set the enemies against themselves causing them to utterly destroy one another without any outside opponent. The people of Judah and Jerusalem, as the Scripture tells us in v.25, had more than enough spoil left behind by their enemies to carry home. In all of this, we learn that "to obey is better than sacrifice, and to hearken than the fat of rams" (1 Samuel 15$^{:22B}$). We must listen and obey God as He speaks to us through His prophets else, we lose the battle, which could come in any form during the course of our life time.

How about the case of Jabez and his kindred, as documented in I Chronicles 4$^{:9-10}$, when they were stricken with abject poverty, and were almost at the point of perishing before he (Jabez) took it upon himself, to fast, and intercede for his people, and as he called upon the name of the Lord? As the Scripture has it, Jabez truly feared God and he had strong faith in God. In other to break the chain of poverty over his family and over his kindred, Jabez had to fast and pray, believing that God is a God of compassion, and of abundance. His prayer was eventually answered, as he persevered and consecrated himself, and his 'coast' was enlarged according to his request and faith in God.

In vv.9 and 10 of I Chronicles Chapter 4, the Scripture tells us as follows: *"And Jabez was more honourable than his brethren: and his mother called his name Jabez, saying, Because I bare him with sorrow. And Jabez called on the God of Isreal, saying, Oh that thou wouldest bless me indeed, and enlarge my coast, and that thine hand might be with me, and that thou wouldest keep me from evil, that it may not grieve me! And God granted him that which he requested"*. Indeed, God sensed the sincerity in Jabez's request, and his steadfastness and faithfulness to Him, and graciously granted it.

Taking a few steps back to the Book of Exodus and as was expressed earlier in this chapter, we read in v.11 of Chapter 34 how God fought several battles for the Israelites, and as He destroyed all the "ites" and "sites" (their enemies) before them on their way to the land of Canaan, the promised land. That miraculous defeat of the enemies of Israel was not without prayer and fasting.

We must endeavor to make some sacrifice sometimes in our lives to stand in the gap and intercede for others, and as we try to bear one another's burden and so fulfill the law of Christ (Galatians 6:2). As God's elects, the need for the presence of our Creator King in our spiritual journey is imperative, and the glory that comes with His presence brings direction, grace and peace which we desperately need to deal with our humanistic limitations.

We must endeavor to make some sacrifice sometimes in our lives to stand in the gap and intercede for others, and as we try to bear one another's burden and so fulfill the law of Christ (Galatians 6:2).

CHAPTER 3

The Body of Christ, And True Discipleship

We begin this chapter by asking the question: What is the Church or who is the Church? The answer to this question is with and within us. The Church represents the Body of Christ, the Ecclesia or those who have been called to do the work of God, and just as the physical body has various parts or members, with each member performing its specific function, so also is the Church. The

The Church represents the Body of Christ, the Ecclesia or those who have been called to do the work of God, and just as the physical body has various parts or members, with each member performing its specific function, so also is the Church.

various auxiliaries or ministries at different levels of authority together constitute the Church. Some people have often misinterpreted, misunderstood, or wrongly defined the Church to be the physical building where people congregate for worship or the four walls where worship and services are held, mostly on Sundays. This misconception must be corrected.

In Matt. 16:18-19, Jesus said to Peter (the leader of His Disciples or the Chief Apostle, as he is otherwise known): *"And I say unto thee, That thou art Peter, and upon this rock I will build my Church, and the gates of hell shall not prevail against it. And I will give unto thee the keys to the kingdom of heaven: and whatsoever thou shall bind on earth shall be bound in heaven: and whatsoever thou shall loose on earth shall be loosed in heaven"*. In other words, Jesus was saying to Peter that on this revelation by the Holy Spirit through him, Peter, He (Jesus) will build His Church and that the gates of hell shall have no power over it.

The Church is indeed God's chosen people who are called by Jesus, and they follow Him. It is made up of those who are committed to Jesus, and who are called to do what He asks them to do; the will of God, and those who have made the same decision Joshua made as he was leading the children of Israel to the Promised Land: *"As for me and my house, we will serve the Lord"*. Peter had the same anointing as Jesus because he, as Jesus, was also filled with the Holy Ghost. Some people have also misconstrued that Jesus is the Church. No, He is not the Church, but instead, He is the Head and we are the Body (the Church), which itself is one foundation.

Regrettably, the Church (the Ecclesia) has continued to perform short of the expectations of its Head, Jesus Christ, and so, has not been able to complete the work of God. This is mostly because, and in most cases, about twenty percent of the Church (the Clergy and or the ordained) are left to do about eighty percent of the work in the Church and thereby, leaving the Church to operate in a pyramidal form. In other words, a few are over-burdened with so much, whereas many within the Body of Christ have done little or nothing to support the Kingdom work. Based on the teachings and operations of Jesus, the Church should be in concentric circles; though He (Jesus) appointed many ministers, He was able to reach out to everybody everywhere.

For the Church to meet the expectations of Jesus, we must address the issue the Apostle Paul pointed out in his message to the Ephesian Church (Ephesians 4). The Body of Christ is one and what defines each of us is the grace God has given to us, but instead of working as one body, we have unwisely divided the Body into two: the clergy and the laity, and we have left the bulk of the work to the former. Keeping aside the five-fold ministry, each member of the Body of Christ is expected to be an evangelist based on the message and instructions of our Lord Jesus as recorded in Mathew 28$^{18\text{-}20}$, where He commanded us to take the Gospel to the uttermost parts of the earth.

True Believers are totally committed to the service of God and are kingdom-centered.

For the purpose of His (Jesus') operation on earth, the Church was established and that purpose is for Jesus' people to govern or to rule and have dominion on earth; hence the term True Discipleship or what Archbishop (Dr.) Joseph A. Alexander refers to as "Christocracy" (meaning the governance of Jesus Christ on earth by His people)[1]. According to Archbishop Alexander, the word "Christocracy" has two components: first, there is "Christo", which comes from the Latin word meaning the Christ, and there is also "Cracy", which relates to government or the governance of the earth. He states that a Christocrat is one who surrenders himself totally to the teaching and practicing of the governance of Jesus Christ on earth. In other words, True Believers are totally committed to the service of God and are kingdom-centered. Therefore, they connect to the greatness of God by His Kingdom and His righteousness in the model of father Abraham, for instance.

Based on its definition, the core of True Discipleship is evangelism as the Scripture tells us in the Gospel According to Saint Matthew Chapter 24, verse 14 (Matt. 24[14]) and Chapter 28, verses 18-20 (Matt. 28[18-20]). The first of these two scriptures states: ***"And this gospel of the kingdom shall be preached throughout the world for a witness to all nations; and then shall the end come"***. The second part of these scriptures, Matt. 28[18-20] is what is referred to as ***the "Great Commission"***, in which our Lord Jesus Christ started by saying that "All power is given to Me in heaven and in earth", and thereafter commissioned His disciples (the True Believers and His followers, or the faithful) and gave us the command to take His teachings and whatsoever we have heard and learned from Him to every part of the earth, and until we do so, His second coming will not occur. It is a global responsibility that has been given to each and every True Believer and should not be limited, by any means, to our little neighborhoods and enclaves nor by anything such as religion, culture, creed, tribe, ethnicity, color, nationality and the like.

This then means that the harvest is indeed plenteous and therefore more laborers like you and I are needed to work in God's vineyard, and as we do so, we must remain steadfast and endure to the end. Remember what the Scripture tells us that no one who puts his hands on the plough and turns back is fit for the Kingdom of God. We must therefore remain faithful, obedient and steadfast in our services for the Kingdom of God.

For the True Disciples, it is no longer us that live but Christ that lives in us, as the Apostle Paul stated. Therefore, a self-centered individual is not fit to practice True Discipleship and indeed, cannot be categorized as a True Disciple. As True Disciples, it is imperative that we fall in love with our Lord Jesus Christ who is the Chief Corner Stone of the Church. In fact, no matter where and when challenges may come from, the True Disciple will remain committed to the cause and the rule of the King of kings, and the Lord of lords. As Jesus' Regents on earth, True Disciples live to protect the interest of Christ the King, and honor his name. As believers, we should know that the Kingdom of God is a system in which our lives are manifested. Therefore God works through his Church, which is the King's Structure for the Kingdom or the Body of Christ: the Church being God's final plan, and the supreme structure of the Kingdom of God.

Although the world is under the bondage of Satan, the Church is not. However, the Church or the Superstructure is not functioning as expected because the power that has been given to her has not worked due to the constant fight with principalities and powers, with the rulers of darkness, and with every ungodly spirit that has ever existed. It is also because of the fact that True Believers have not come to the full understanding of God's purpose, and in which case we miss our priorities. God created us in his own image, and then instructed us to increase, multiply, and replenish the earth, and to rule or govern and take dominion. This is the mandate God gave to us and the purpose for which we are created. Therefore, making God's priorities our priorities, and aligning our plans with God's plan is what True Discipleship entails. We, the Body of Christ (the Church or the Ecclesia), are called for the purpose of advancing the Kingdom of God to the spheres of humanity. And one may ask; what is the Kingdom of God? The Bible tells us that the Kingdom of God is love, peace and joy in the Holy Ghost. It is longsuffering, gentleness, goodness, meekness and temperance, and the Scripture also tells us in Galatians 5:25B that *"against such there is no law"*.

We must not lose sight of the fact that our Heavenly Father (God) is bound by His principles, and we must understand the revelation we have in the present day as seen in Hebrew 2:5, which reads: *"For to the angels has He not put in subjection the world to come, whereof we speak"*. As True Disciples, we must face confrontation, and we must deal with the challenges of this world. The primary aspect of True Discipleship is that we must be faithfully fruitful in all our dealings.

In Matt. 28:18-20, Jesus spoke to his eleven disciples (with Judas Iscariot out of the picture at that time) and said *"All power is given unto me in heaven and in earth. Go ye therefore, and teach all nations, baptizing them in the name of the Father, and of the Son, and of the Holy Ghost: Teaching them to observe all things whatsoever I have commanded you: and, lo, I am with you alway, even unto the end of the world"*.

The Gospel of Jesus Christ according to Saint Mark 16:15-18 provided a more detailed version of this transfer of power and authority from Jesus to us, the True Disciples. Beginning from v.15, Jesus said: *"Go ye into the world, and preach the gospel to every creature. He that believeth and is baptized shall be saved, but he that believeth not shall be damned. And these signs shall follow them that believe; In my name shall they cast out devils; they shall speak with new tongues; They shall take up serpents; and if they drink any deadly thing, it shall not hurt them; they shall lay hands on the sick, and they shall recover"*. Otherwise referred to as the Great Commission, this handing-over of divine power and authority by Jesus to Jesus' People or believers, is the center of True Discipleship, that is, the rulership or governance of Jesus' People for Jesus on planet earth. The ultimate goal of True Discipleship is to bring the Kingdom of God to the spheres of humanity, and every True Disciple must be determined to accomplish this goal. The True Discipleship belief is that humanity should be prepared to have the privilege to enter the Kingdom of God.

To be a True Disciple means to be solely and completely committed to the work of God, and he/she is one who is completely committed to the purpose and rulership of Jesus Christ here on earth. He/she is someone who works according to the plan, priority and purpose of God or as a Regent of The Christ. Thus, True Disciples are those who have been called and spiritually positioned to govern, to rule, and to establish the dominion glory on earth. They are part of the solution and are not, and should not be additions to the world problems.

"Daraprim Christians" (the "Sunday, Sunday medicine Christians")2, the Christmas-New Year-Easter Church goers, and any other similar non-practicing Christians are excluded in the definition of True Disciples

Inevitably, the governing and ruling, with respect to True Discipleship, will not happen unless we take our princely positions as stated in John 20:[22B-23] which says: "receive ye the Holy Ghost: Whosoever sins ye remit, they are remitted unto them: and whosoever

32

sins ye retain, they are retained". It must be clearly stated that the "Daraprim Christians" (the "Sunday, Sunday medicine Christians")[2], the Christmas-New Year-Easter Church goers, and any other similar non-practicing Christians are excluded in the definition of True Disciples, since they are not qualified as such. One thing we must bear in mind is the fact that by definition, every True Disciple is a Christian, but not everyone that calls himself/herself a Christian is a True Disciple; there is a big difference between these two.

Going back to Chapter 6 of the Gospel according to Saint Mark, the Scripture tells us in vv.6-7 that Jesus called unto him the twelve disciples, and began to send them forth by two and two; and gave them power over unclean spirits; And commanded them that they should take nothing for their journey, save a staff, only; no script, no bread, and no money in their purse. In v.11 of this same Scripture, Jesus instructed the disciples saying "And whosoever shall not receive you, nor hear you, when you depart thence, shake-off the dust under your feet for a testimony against them".

God called us, ordained us, made us His regents and co-heirs to the Throne with Jesus Christ, and then commissioned us in what is known as the "Great Commission" that we should go and teach all nations; *"baptizing them in the name of the Father, and of the Son, and of the Holy Ghost; Teaching them to observe all things whatsoever I have commanded you; and lo, I am with you alway, even unto the end of the world"* (Matt. 28:19-20). This means that we should not be selfish over our salvation, which of course was given unto us freely. God gave us a mandate and then provided us with the wherewithal we will need to carry it out.

Similarly, in Revelation 5:9B-10, the Scripture says of the Master and the believers as follows: *"for you were slain and have redeemed us to God by your blood out of every tribe and tongue and people and nation, and have made us kings and priests to our God; and we shall reign on the earth"*. The ending part of this Scripture makes it clear that the rulership of this earth is in the hands of the Believers, since we have been made kings and priests, and where the king resides is otherwise called his kingdom. We are therefore called and given the power to govern and to take dominion over all forces of darkness, over all rulers of darkness, over all principalities and powers, and over every ungodly spirit that ever existed.

The mandate of dominion is given to the believer. Therefore, the believer must be fully persuaded that the glory of God is within him/her. We must therefore not hesitate to exercise the power and authority that has been bestowed upon us as the chosen ones to govern and to rule this earth. The believer must live demonstrably of who he/she is before the eyes of the enemy. In other words, believers must fully identify themselves as they confront the enemy, and he (the enemy) knows that He that is in you (the believer) is greater than him. 1 Peter 2:9 identifies the believers as "a chosen generation, a royal priesthood, an holy nation, a peculiar people". In the later part of this same Scripture, the Apostle Peter adds that the believer "should show forth the praises of him who hath called you out of darkness into the marvelous light".

As the called, God wants us to do his desires. In v.15 of Chapter 8 the Gospel of Jesus Christ according to Saint John, our Lord Jesus Christ said: "Herein is my Father glorified, that ye bear much fruit; so shall ye be my disciples". God said that we should keep His Commandments if we love Him. Three times, Jesus asked Simon Peter: "Do you love me? When Peter answered Him saying: "Lord you know I love you", Jesus said to Him: "Feed my sheep". This statement, though may sound very simple, is very comprehensive and deep in meaning. By telling Peter to feed His sheep, Jesus was indeed telling Peter to prepare believers to rule, and to take dominion.

Jesus said that He calls His sheep and they hear him and follow Him. The willingness and commitment to obey God completely is what True Discipleship is all about. In Jn. 15:1-2 Jesus said *"I am the true vine, and my Father is the husbandman. Every branch in me that beareth not fruit he taketh away: and every branch that beareth fruit, he purgeth it, that it may bring forth more fruit"*. In v.5 He (Jesus) said: *"I am the true vine, ye are the branches. He that abideth in me, and I in him, the same bringeth forth much fruit: for without me you can do nothing"*. He went further to say in v.7 of this same section of the Gospel that *"If ye abide in me, and my words abide in you, ye shall ask what ye will, and it shall be done unto you"*. In fact, in Chapter 15 of His Gospel according to Saint John, Jesus stressed His union with the Church, and in some cases, using parables to illustrate that relationship.

In the Acts of the Holy Ghost in the life of the Apostles, otherwise known as the Acts of the Apostles, Acts 1:8 Jesus instructed His eleven disciples on the day of His Ascension (the Ascension Day) saying: *"But ye shall receive power after that the Holy Ghost be come upon you; and you shall be witnesses unto me both in Jerusalem, and in Judea, and in Samaria, and unto the uttermost part of the earth".* This instruction of Jesus to His disciples represented a promise of Spiritual equipment for worldwide campaign and evangelism.

The phrase *"after the Holy Ghost is come upon you"* is a very powerful and divine statement because without the gift of the power of the Holy Spirit, the disciples would be incapable of casting out any demon nor be able to heal the sick and set the captives free as they did afterwards, starting with the healing of the lame man at the gate called The Beautiful. Jesus also said that greater works than these, (that is, the miraculous works he did in their presence), ye shall do, meaning that they will do more than He did because the gift of the the Holy Ghost they will receive will bring exponentiation and amplification of the works that they (you and I) will do afterwards.

As True Believers, and those who have been called and anointed to live according to God's plan, purpose and priority, we must not hold our peace in challenging the unbelivers to repentance by living for Christ. We must stand for the Church, the Body of Christ (the Superstructure) and intercede with perseverance for the ungodly and for the lost souls, and we can only do this through prayer and fasting, and as we draw nearer to God.

Indeed, the comprehensive duties of a true believer can best be summarized from the Mission Statement of the New Covenant Christian Ministries Worldwide (headquartered in The Bronx, New York, USA) as follows:

❖ Preparing Christ dominion-centered believers to bring the Kingdom of God to the sphere of humanity;

❖ Teaching the full counsel of God's revelation as taught and demonstrated by Christ to change human thinking;

❖ Exercising the authority of the Kingdom of Christ on earth; and

❖ Aggressively advancing the kingdom of Christ to the end of the earth.

In any event, as True Disciples of Jesus we must understand that we are God's chosen generation, born to show His excellence, and from all that God has given us, we must know who we are. In other words, even though we dwell in this world, we must realize that we are not of the world. To remain or live as an unbeliever is to be spiritually blind and spiritually ignorant. As the Scripture tells us in I Corinthians 2:14, the unbeliever, otherwise referred to as the natural man, do not receive the things of the Spirit of God: for they are foolishness unto him; neither can he know them, because they are spiritually discerned.

In the Tenth Chapter of the Gospel according to Saint Luke vv. 17-24, we are told that the seventy who Jesus appointed and sent two by two on a mission returned with gladness and said to Him, "Lord even the demons submit to us in your name", and He replied, "I saw Satan fall like lightning from heaven". Jesus continued and said to them, "I have given you authority to trample on snakes and scorpions and to overcome all the power of the enemy; nothing will harm you." **He then cautioned them and said;** *"However, do not rejoice that the spirits submit to you, but rejoice that your names are written in heaven."* Finally, Jesus, after He returned to His disciples (vv. 23-24) said privately to them, "Blessed are the eyes that see what you see. For I tell you that many prophets and kings wanted to see what you see but did not see it, and hear what you hear but did not hear it."

One thing we must understand is the fact that Spiritual authority is not given to everyone. It is rather given to those who have truly received Jesus and believe in Him, and love Him by obeying His Commandments. For as many as have received Him, to them He has given the power to become the sons of God (John 1:12).

CHAPTER 4

The Spiritual, Physical and Socioeconomic Benefits of Fasting and Prayer

When we make fasting and prayer a part of our regular living, we become better equipped spiritually to withstand all trials and tribulations, temptations and wiles of the enemy, and indeed, we become better positioned to pass any test when we are tested.

First and foremost, fasting, particularly corporate dry fasting is spiritually rejuvenating. Spiritually speaking, fasting and prayer tend to give us the spiritual sanity that we so desire, and help to strengthen us in our daily walk towards spiritual maturity. When we make fasting and prayer a part of our regular living, we become better equipped spiritually to withstand all trials and tribulations, temptations and wiles of the enemy, and indeed, we become better positioned to pass any test when we are tested.

For our spiritual growth, we must steadfastly have fellowship with God since the lack of fellowship with Him makes us vulnerable to sin. It is imperative, therefore, that when we fast and pray that we do so with good intentions and for the right causes if we expect to reap the divine benefits of fasting. In the Gospel according to Saint Matthew Chapter 6, v.24, our Lord Jesus, in His teachings during the Sermon on the Mount, said clearly to His disciples that: "No man can serve two masters; for either he will hate the one, and love the other; or else he will hold to the one, and despise the other". In other words, as true disciples of Jesus Christ, we cannot "serve God and mammon" at the same time; else we deceive ourselves.

A major spiritual benefit of fasting is sanctification. When we fast and pray, we consecrate or make ourselves holy before God through spiritual purification and cleansing, while setting ourselves apart, and free from sin.

A major spiritual benefit of fasting is sanctification. When we fast and pray, we consecrate or make ourselves holy before God through spiritual purification and cleansing, while setting ourselves apart, and free from sin. Of course, we have proof of sanctification through fasting and prayer since we now are able to possess or have full control of our bodies in holiness. Overall, and as the elect of God, we become close to God.

In Isaiah 58, God made it clear that He will not listen to our cry when we fast and pray and we do so with wickedness and ungodly intentions. Let us revisit this Scripture which is very familiar to most of us. Beginning from v.4 and ending in v.12, God said:

'Behold ye fast for strife and debate, and to smite with the fist of wickedness: ye shall not fast as you do this day, to make your voice heard on high. Is such a fast that I have chosen? a day for a man to afflict his soul? Wilt thou call this a fast, and an acceptable day of the Lord? Is not this the fast that I have chosen? to loose the bands of wickedness, to undo the heavy burdens, and to let the oppressed go free, and that ye break every yoke? Is it not to deal thy bread to the hungry, and that thou bring the poor that are cast out of thy house?

When thou seest the naked, that thou covered him: and that thou hide not thyself from thine own flesh? Then shall thy light break forth as the morning, and thine health shall spring forth speedily: and thy righteousness shall go before thee; the glory of the Lord shall be thy rearward (or rear guard). *Then shall thou call, and the Lord shall answer; thou shall cry, and he shall say here, Here I am. If thou shall take away from the mist of thee the yoke, and putting forth of the finger, and speaking vanity; And if thou draw out thy soul to the hungry, and satisfy the afflicted soul; then shall thy light rise in obscurity, and thy darkness be as the noonday:* **And the Lord shall guide thee continually, and satisfy thy soul in drought, and make fat thy bones: and thou shalt be like watered**

garden, and like a spring of water, whose waters fail not. *And they that shall be of thee shall build the old waste places: thou shalt raise up the foundations of many generations;* **and thou shall be called The Repairer of the breach, The Restorer of paths to dwell in**.

Moving forward to the Book of Daniel, we see a clear manifestation of the benefits of fasting and prayers in action. When Daniel was identified as the only one in the land who could interpret King Nebuchadnezzar's dream, the Scripture tells us in Daniel 2^{17-18} that Daniel *"went to his house and made the thing known to Hananiah (Shadrach), Mihael (Meshach), and Azariah (Abednego), his companions: That they would desire mercies of the God of heaven concerning this secret; that Daniel and his fellows should not perish with the rest of the wise men of Babylon"*. The Scripture also tells us in v.19 that at the end of their solemn assembly and fasting, the secret was revealed to Daniel in a night vision by an angel of the Lord; and he *"blessed the God of heaven"*.

In vv. 47-48 of the Chapter 2 of Daniel, the Scripture says that *"the king* (meaning King Nebuchadnezzar) *answered unto Daniel, and said,* **of a truth it is, that your God is a God of gods, and a Lord of kings, and a revealer of secrets**, *seeing thou couldest reveal this secret"*. Consequently, Daniel was promoted by King Nebuchadnezzar according to his promise. In v.48, the Scripture says: *"Then the king made Daniel a great man, and gave him many great gifts, and made him ruler over the whole province of*

Babylon and chief of the governors over all the wise men of Babylon". This elevation of Daniel from a little known Hebrew boy who was taken captive, to the Governor of governors did not happen by his own ability or strength. Rather, it happened as the result of his steadfast prayer and fasting, as well as his faithfulness and obedience to God, and as he established a very intimate relationship with Him.

Furthermore, recall the story of Joseph and Potiphar's wife in Genesis Chapter 39. This story, which is very familiar to many believers, has a powerful message embedded in it. Now, just remember that when Joseph was tested in Pharaoh's Palace through Potiphar's wife, the Ten Commandments, which were given in Exodus Chap. 20, have not even been written. Moses the Law Giver has not even started to lead the children of Israel at that time, and even though he, Joseph, was in the position of power to do whatsoever he wanted to do and then have a cover-up afterwards, he was very much able to resist all the temptations and at the end passed the test that was put before him. Remember, and as the Scripture tells us, that Joseph was next to Pharaoh, and was the second in command in the Government of Egypt as of that time. He was also Pharaoh's adopted son and the prince, based on what the Scripture tells us.

What then do we think made Joseph not to succumb, yield, or fall victim to this temptation when he could have yielded to Potiphar's wife's request to commit adultery with her, and knowing that she had so much "crush" on him? The relationship Joseph developed with God, and which he continued to hold strongly through fasting and prayer throughout his life time was the key reason behind this power to overcome temptations.

Let's again read Joseph's response to Potiphar's wife as she approached him, and as recorded in Gen. 39:8-9. The Scripture says: *"But he refused, and said unto his master's wife, Behold, my master wotteth not what is with me in the house,* **and he had committed all that he hath to my hand: There is none greater in this house than I; neither hath he kept back anything from me but thee, because thou art his wife;** *how then can I do this great wickedness, and sin against God?"*

In fact, the tenacity and perseverance of Potiphar's wife to get Joseph to commit the sin of adultery with her was over-shadowed by the anointing upon him, and his faithfulness to God, as well as the fact that he feared God greatly, as the Scripture tells us. In verse 10 of Gen. 39, we read that *"And as it came to pass, as she (Potiphar's wife) spoke to Joseph day by day, that he hearkened not unto her to lie by her, or to be with her."*

One of the outstanding physical benefits (otherwise referred to as the side or unintentional effects) of fasting is body weight loss and if you are one of the doubting thomases among us, try it and see for yourself. Turning our plates and dishes upside down and taking away our minds from food and shoving gluttony, and saying see you later to "king stomach" for at least once a one day over a week will no doubt make a difference in our body weight and lateral size.

Biologically speaking, as we cease to grow vertically, usually in our early or mid-twenties, as the case may be, our body will start to experience lateral or sideways growth, thereby resulting in bigger bellies or "pot bellies" (as some would call it), in some cases, and wider waist lines, for instance.

Aligning with the above is the fact that fasting helps to flush our intestinal system, and also reduces the stress our digestive organs encounter during the biological process of catabolism and anabolism associated with the digestive system as we stuff our bodies with excess food substances. We sometimes subject our bodies to some physical discomforts (or disutility, as it is termed in economics) and bring demise to ourselves in the process. This becomes even more pronounced if we are one of those frequent patrons of fast food restaurants and who always love to super-size their orders. Literarily, it is synonymous to periodically flushing the sewer lines in order to avoid back-ups and the physical and financial damages they cause.

Of course, the physical benefits we experience as a result of fasting translates into economic and social gains ranging from the fee we pay at the gym or to belong to a health club, to the savings we enjoy from not buying new clothing. We may need to change our wardrobes since our bodies' lateral growth is now being indirectly controlled or put in check. In addition, there are savings on grocery shopping, and on cooking gas bills, etc., and of course some relief on our refrigerators.

Furthermore, there are savings on our water and sewage bills due to the obvious reduced visits to the toilet as "king stomach" continues to have less and less waste materials to offer or surrender to the sewer lines, and as the fast progresses, particularly in the case of the dry (extreme) fast and the normal fast. In other words, fasting creates more opportunity for us to make more visits to the House of Praise and less visits to the house of waste (a.k.a. toilet). (For those of us who are not aware of this fact, each time we use the toilet, we generate what is known as a "combo-bill" for the water and the sewage, and which of course excludes the price we pay per visit for the toilet paper.)

Together, these savings frees up some money or financial resources for us thereby, giving us more purchasing power and the power to sow more seeds to enable the advancement of God's work. We must understand the obvious fact that these benefits as well as others that have not been herein mentioned are meant for those who whole heartedly commit themselves to, and persevere in the observation of the fast all through the period, as proclaimed, without any lukewarm, disobedience spirit, and unfaithfulness as to the specificities guiding the fast.

Overall, it is either we want to fast and do it right or we don't; there is no case of go in between in this solemn matter since God hates a lukewarm attitude, and will spit you out if you are neither hot nor cold. We must be diligent, and we must persevere, for our God rewards those who diligently seek Him. Speaking of being diligent and remaining steadfast as we seek and serve the Lord, and as we conclude this chapter, it is imperative that we read what the Scriptures say in Isaiah 61:4-11, and 62:2-12. Believe it or not, the promises of God spoken in those Scriptures (and indeed in the rest of the Scriptures) will surely come to pass unto the true believers; for He is the Alpha and the Omega, and His words are yeah and amen.

Signs, Wonders, Miracles and Testimonies

When we fully position ourselves spiritually through fasting and prayers, and as we take dominion over the earth, signs and wonders follow thereafter, and the Scriptures affirm this in several instances. The Bible tells us that we overcome by the Blood of the Lamb and the words of our testimonies. Therefore, it is very necessary that we testify God's goodness to us whenever we experience one.

When we fully position ourselves spiritually through fasting and prayers, and as we take dominion over the earth, signs and wonders follow thereafter, and the Scriptures affirm this in several instances.

Several signs and wonders were reported or witnessed during and after the November-December 2011, and the October-December 2012 Fasting and Prayer sessions at the New Covenant Christian Ministries in New York City based on the testimonies given by those who fully participated in those eventful gatherings of the Saints. Although miracles, signs and wonders were experienced and reported during the two seasons of fasting and prayers, the focus here is on the 2012 Forty Days Fast.

At the end of **the October 28 – December 6, 2012 Forty Days Fast**, which was originally proclaimed for twenty-one days, and later extended, several testimonies of miraculous works were given by those who actively participated in the event. (Please understand that for the sake of confidentiality, the names of the individuals associated with the following testimonies of miracles have been withheld.) Prominent among these testimonies as noted and summarized include that:

- One of the pastors in the Ministry testified of his father being healed from the affliction of cancer cells, which lingered in his body for several months without cure.
- The daughter of one of the ordained ministers received her immigrant visa after twelve years of constant denial by the United States Immigration and Naturalization Services (INS).
- A female member of the Church reported the release of her son from the hospital in New York City after a long period of hospitalization.
- An ordained servant of the Lord testified of a financial breakthrough she received from God through her job after being terminated (fired or sacked) by the same employer some

months earlier. Judging from the tithe this servant of God paid later, it is believed that the breakthrough was quite substantial, and indeed significant.

Several other testimonies of a lesser magnitude, however, were given as people continued to experience the goodness of God, while remaining faithful and steadfast in the Lord during the fasting season as observed. Most importantly, many individuals gave their lives to Christ, as they were spiritually moved by the Word of God and the testimonies which they heard during the daily and nightly gatherings throughout that Holy Ghost-filled season. Indeed, the experiences from those fasting seasons could be likened to the activities of the Day of Pentecost, as recorded in the Acts of the Holy Spirit in the lives of the Apostles, otherwise known as the Acts of the Apostles.

The Scripture focus for the 2012 solemn assembly was taken from John 15:8, which says: *Herein is my Father glorified, that ye may bear much fruit; so shall ye be my disciples"*. Those who were fully and completely "souled out" to God during those solemn assemblies felt the glory of the Lord shown around them, and as they became saturated with His divine anointing. Here, we present some of the highlights of the activities that were observed during those eventful and memorable seasons.

Day One Through To Day Forty

As we journeyed through grace and glory every day of those solemn forty days and forty nights, the saints became saturated with divine anointing, as the glory of the Lord rose among us. Again, the overall focus of the fasting and prayer as previously expressed was extracted from John 15:8, which says: *"Herein is my Father glorified, that ye bear much fruit; so shall ye be my disciples"*. The theme and the prayer focus on the first day (October 28) of the 2012 solemn gatherings was: "Knowing Your Source" and the Scripture reference was taken from the Gospel according to Saint John, Chapter 15, and verse 1 (John 15:1) where Jesus said *"I am the true vine and my Father is the husbandman"*. Here, the union between Christ and his Church is expressed and clearly explained, and our prayer in this case is that the Lord will help us to acknowledge him as our only source of existence, as well as the Author and Finisher of our faith.

On Day Two of the gatherings, the prayer focus was on "Purging and Purification", and the Church prayed that the Lord will purge us (the Body of Christ) that we may bring forth more fruit. The Scripture reference was taken from John 15:2 where our Lord Jesus spoke to us and said: *"Every branch in me that beareth not fruit he taketh away: and every branch that beareth fruit, he purgeth it, that it may bear forth more fruit"*.

From Day Three through Day Five, the prayer focus was on "Spiritual Cleansing and Abiding in the Lord", and the Church prayed that the Lord will cleanse us through his Word, and to enable us to abide in him. The Scripture references for those three gracious days of solemn assembly were extracted from John 15:3-6, which read as follows: *"Now ye are clean through the word which I have spoken unto you. Abide in me, and I in you, as the branch cannot bear fruit of itself, except it abide in the vine; no more can ye, except ye abide in me. I am the vine, ye are the branches: He that abideth in me, and I in him, the same bringeth forth much fruit: for without me, you can do nothing. If a man abides not in me, he is cast forth as a branch, and is withered; and men gather them, and cast them into the fire, and they are burned"*.

As the spiritual walk with the Lord continued, and as the Church proceeded from Day Six through Day Forty, transformation of many of the faithful was observed, as many believers started to actually walk in the Spirit.

The Day After

On, the day after the forty days of fasting and prayers, victory celebration was the order of the day as testimonies of miracles, signs and wonders were given by True Believers and others that faithfully responded to the call for a solemn assembly, and who steadfastly participated in the fast for the entire season. The Scripture meditation for that remarkable day was taken from John 11:1-45 which focused on one of the greatest miracles Jesus performed while on earth: Calling the dead Lazarus back to life.

In John 11:4, the Scripture tells us thus; *"When Jesus heard that (Lazarus was dead), He said, this sickness is not to death, but for the glory of God, that the Son of God might be glorified thereby"*. In v.11 of the same Scripture, Jesus spoke to His disciples and said to them, *"Our friend Lazarus sleeps; but I go, that I may awake him out of sleep"*. But in v.14 -15, he plainly said to the same disciples, *"Lazarus is dead. And I am glad for your sakes that I was not there, to the intent you may believe; nevertheless let us go to him"*. When Martha (the sister of Lazarus) said to Jesus (in John 11:24), *"I know that he (Lazarus) shall rise again in resurrection at the last day"*, Jesus said to her (in vv.25-26), **I am the resurrection, and the life, he that believes in Me, though he were dead; yet shall he live: And whosoever lives and believes in Me, shall never die.** Believe you this?"

In fact, Martha's bold response to Jesus' specific question on this very issue is a major factor in accomplishing the Lord's miracle of bringing her brother, Lazarus back to life. Those that believe in Jesus will no doubt see the glory of the Lord manifest in their lives. The Scripture in John 11:45 finally concluded on this particular miraculous work of Jesus and said; *"Then many of the Jews which came to Mary, and had seen the things which Jesus did, believed on Him"*. These Jews believed because they witnessed the event, but Jesus told His disciples in John 20:29B saying; *"blessed are they that have not seen, and yet have believed"*. The Scripture also tells us that without faith, it is impossible to serve God. Martha had faith that Jesus is able to do that which is impossible with men, and her brother came back to life because she believed even before the miracle took place.

The First Sunday After

This particular day could otherwise be captioned "The Special Day of Testimonies". It was a glorious day that was over-flowing with praise, worship and adoration to the Almighty God for His goodness and mercy, and for the great things He had done.

On the first Sunday following the Forty Days Fast, several testimonies were given by those who participated and benefited from the solemn gathering and program. Some of the highlights of the day included testimonies given by some ministers including pastors. A Senior Pastor testified of how God miraculously saved her from a serious car accident. A special thanksgiving was given by a sister as she testified of the healing miracle she experienced during the fast. (This ordained servant of the Lord was diagnosed with the extreme case of high blood pressure but without any medical help, her blood pressure miraculously normalized during the fast.)

Similarly, another sister (a servant of the Lord) testified of how God miraculously used her to save the reputation of the healthcare facility where she worked. According to her testimony, the healthcare facility was over-whelmed with numerous citations for violations of government healthcare regulations from the agency that watches and regulates the operations of such healthcare facilities. Overall, the atmosphere was filled with the glory of the Lord, and the Body of Christ felt as it was indeed on the Day of the Pentecost.

CHAPTER 5

Covenanting With God And Walking in The Spirit

Covenanting With God

In many sections of the Old Testament Scriptures, we read about many men and women of God and how they covenanted with God, with Abraham, the "father of faith", being the prominent among them. The covenant made between God and Abraham is one of the most powerful covenants recorded in the Bible. The Bible also reveals to us how God made covenant with the children of Israel, time and time again even as they lived a stubborn and disobedient life.

When King Solomon finished building the house of the Lord, and the king's house (his house), the Lord appeared to him by night and said unto him, *"I have heard thy prayer, and have chosen this place for myself for* *an house of sacrifice. **If I shut up heaven that there be no rain, or if I command the locusts to devour the land, or if I send pestilence among my people; If only my people who are called by my name will humble themselves, and pray and seek My face and turn from their wicked ways,** then I will hear from heaven, and will forgive their sin and heal their land*" (II Chronicles 7:12-14). In other words, God will always keep His own part of the covenant with us if we keep ours.

We must never forget to do those things which are pleasing to God, and to ask for his forgiveness when we break His Commandments, and offend Him. King Solomon, even though God had chosen him to build

> *We must never forget to do those things which are pleasing to God, and to ask for his forgiveness when we break His Commandments, and offend Him.*

His temple, there were so many evils committed in Israel, including those by the king himself during his reign. We may recall that God chose King Solomon instead of his father and predecessor, King David to build the temple for Him because He (God) said that the hands of the later were too bloody and therefore unfit to build His house.

Assuredly, all the Ten Commandments are summarized in the first two commandments, with the very first of these two being the greatest commandment: *"Thou shall love the Lord thy God with all thy heart, with all thy soul, and with all thy strength. Love thy neighbor as thy self."* Within these two commandments rest the other eight commandments, because whom you love you would not harm nor have any evil thoughts towards that person. You would do unto that person the way you would want others do or relate to you. If we love God, it means that we must trust Him, obey His Commandments, and remain faithful to Him. God demands an honest, exclusive, wholehearted, and undivided allegiance and devotion to Him from us. James 4:10 says: *"Humble yourself in the sight of the Lord and He shall lift you up"*.

Walking in The Spirit

The presence of God in our lives rescues us from the evils of all principalities and powers, and gives us the peace and calmness we need in the midst of all the hustle and bustle we experience daily here on earth. The letter of the Apostle Paul to the Galatian Church as recorded in Galatians Chapter 5, vv. 16-26, explains to us what it means to walk in the Spirit.

> *The presence of God in our lives rescues us from the evils of all principalities and powers, and gives us the peace and calmness we need in the midst of all the hustle and bustle we experience daily here on earth.*

Throughout Chapter 5 of his letter to the Galatians, the Apostle Paul stressed on the liberty of the believers. He emphasized that the believers having been called to liberty, are free to resist their sinful nature. He added that as they follow the leading of the Holy Spirit and crucify the passions and lusts of the flesh, the fruit of the Holy Spirit should and will be seen in their lives. The Scripture tells us in Romans 8:1 that: *"There is therefore no condemnation to them which are in Christ Jesus, who walk not after the flesh, but after the Spirit".*

In v.16 of Galatians 5, which is the core of his message, Saint Paul discussed why those who have been saved by grace are able to have a changed life and love one another by walking in the Spirit. To walk in the Spirit means to live as the Holy Spirit would have us live, i.e., to put on the whole armor of God or to live by the nine fruit of the Holy Spirit every moment of our life. It means to say that we must be willing to put our lives at risk in order to save it. We need to get out of ourselves and be connected with God. This could involve re-arranging things in our lives to ensure that the work of God is done and as we do so, God will in turn re-order things in our lives for them to work well.

In all his dealings, and even while going through trials and tribulations, Saint Paul never lost sense of who he is nor forgot the essence of what God wanted him to do. He was relentlessly enthusiastic and in fact remained focused at the center of his relationship with God. In vv.10-11 of Chapter 3 of his letter to the Christians of the Church in Philistia (Philippians 3:10-11), Apostle Paul stated as follows: *"that I may know Him and the power of His resurrection, and the fellowship of His sufferings, being conformed to His death; If by any means, I might attain unto the resurrection of the dead."* Continuing in v.14 of this same Scripture, the Apostle added the following statement: *I press toward the mark for the prize of the high calling of God in Christ Jesus"*. There is no doubt that Saint Paul, the Great Apostle, was a good role model for every believer, and he lived a life that we must all emulate, if indeed we must remain able laborers in God's vineyard.

Truth and faith must be balanced if we are to remain with God, and to continue to live as laborers in His vineyard. We must endeavor to allow God's truth to transform our lives. When we do so, we gain much more than what we expect from Him. As God works with us in the inside, we must work on the external view where God said that He will put His Spirit within us and cause us to walk in His statutes. Clearly stated, the reason for salvation is that God has a plan for us, to use us to show forth His strength and authority and to communicate the love He has for the lost community.

We must therefore endeavor to sanctify ourselves and, indeed, remain sanctified in order for God to "make the place of our feet glorious" as He has promised us in Isaiah 60:13. **For those who tend to support immoral lifestyles, be it known to you that although one may argue that we live in the age of moral decadence, we must understand the gospel truth that no moral wrong can ever be a civil right.**

In 2 Peter 1:5-9 Simon Peter (Apostle Peter) encourages us on how we should live in order to escape the corruption in the world caused by evil desires. Beginning from the fifth verse, he said: *"For this reason, make every effort to add to your faith, goodness; and to goodness, knowledge; and to knowledge, self-control; and to self-control, perseverance; and to perseverance, godliness; and to godliness, mutual affection; and to mutual affection, love"*. He then said: ***"For if you possess these qualities in increasing measure, they will keep you from being ineffective and unproductive in your knowledge of our Lord Jesus Christ.*** *But whoever does not have them is nearsighted and blind, forgetting that they have been cleansed from their past sins".*

When we steadfastly walk in the Spirit, we will see visions and dream dreams, and God will give us the wisdom to interpret our own dreams. Vision is indeed the central driving force of a man. It represents what God can do while dream is what we can do. When we fellowship with God, it enhances our potential to seek, knock, ask and find because we already have direct access to Him and are therefore, no strangers to Him. We must develop the attitude of meeting God and reverencing Him whenever we come before His holy presence (His Throne of Grace).

When we steadfastly walk in the Spirit, we will see visions and dream dreams, and God will give us the wisdom to interpret our own dreams.

The Psalmist, in Psalm 23:6, says: *"Surely goodness and mercy shall follow me all the days of my life; and I will dwell in the house of the LORD forever"*. We must understand that the blessings and benefits contained in this Psalm will not go to everybody. Rather, it is meant for those who come to Jesus Christ, the Shepherd. In other words they are meant for the sheep who hear the

Shepherd as He calls them and follow Him. Recall that v.1 of this same Psalm says "The Lord is my Shepherd, I shall not want." Therefore, if the Lord is our Shepherd, we must listen and follow Him by doing what He wants us to do, and do so without grudges and hesitation, but to faithfully do so with humility and reverence. As the Shepherd, Jesus reminds us in John 10:27, and said: *"My sheep hear My voice, and I know them, and they follow Me"*. Again, the Scripture tells us in Romans 8:14 that: *"For as many as are led by the Spirit of God, they are the sons of God"*.

God is so gracious to us and He has proven this over and over again. In Ezekiel 36:24-30, God spoke to the children of Israel clearly and said: *"For I will take you from among the heathen, and gather you out of countries, and will bring you into your own land. Then I will sprinkle clean water upon you, and you shall be clean: from all your filthiness, and from all your idols, will I cleanse you. A new heart will I give you, and a new spirit will I put within you: and I will take away the stony heart out of your flesh, and I will give you a heart of flesh. And I will put my spirit within you, and cause you to walk in my statutes, and you shall keep my judgments and do them. And you shall dwell in the land that I gave to your fathers; and you shall be my people, and I will be your God. I will also save you from all uncleanliness: and I will call for the corn, and will increase it, and lay no famine upon you. And I will multiply the fruit of the tree and the increase of the field, that ye shall receive no more reproach of famine among the heathen"*. Furthermore, in Ezekiel 37:26, God added unto His assurances and said: *Moreover, I will make a covenant of peace with them (the Israelites); it shall be an everlasting covenant with them; and I will place them, and multiply them, and will set my sanctuary in the midst of them for evermore".*

Know this, sin creates a barrier between us and God and therefore, it separates us from Him. Just as Judas Iscariot who betrayed Jesus for thirty pieces of silver felt so guilty at the Communion Table during that Last Super, and so guilty that his conscience could not allow him to neither eat the bread (which symbolizes the Body of Christ that was sacrificed for our sins) nor drink the fruit of the vine (which symbolizes the Blood of Christ which He shed for the remission of our sins). When our hearts are pure with God, we feel very comfortable to be in His presence, because those who come to Him must do so with holiness, purity, sincerity, and with reverence. May God help us to speak to others in a way that will help them see Him in us so that He will be glorified. As we sing, as we talk, as we teach, and as we preach the Word, may God be seen in us so that He (God) will draw men unto Him and thereby be glorified.

Indeed, as we become saved, the Holy Spirit comes and dwells in us. He gives our spirit a new birth and in that Spirit, we have everlasting life. However, our resurrected soul lives in a body that still has the lust of flesh. But the good news is that we can overcome this spiritual warfare by following the leading of the Holy Spirit. We were once buried in sins but Jesus located us, picked us up and cleansed us from all our sins and unrighteousness. When the Lord heals you and restores you, you must take dominion and move forward in the Spiritual realm. We live by the Grace of God each day of our life; hence we are no longer under the law.

The law came to increase the knowledge of sin, but we are no longer under the law but under the grace of God. The Apostle Paul discussed this very point in a more detailed approach in Chapter 8:11-14 of his letter to the Church in Rome (Romans 8:11-14). As the Scripture warns us, if we continue to satisfy the lust of the flesh, then, it means that we don't have the Spirit in us; meaning that we are not of Christ. The end point of this is eternal death in hell fire on the Judgment Day, and that is whether or not we believe it. Hence the Scripture in Hebrews 9:27 tells us that *"it is once appointed unto man to die and after that, judgment"*.

In v.17 of Galatians 5, the Apostle Paul stressed that the lust of our sinful body and the leading of the Holy Spirit are entirely opposed to each other. While our body is in total rebellion against God, our born again spirit is in agreement with the Holy Spirit. This means that a born again Christian's life is indeed a battle,

The law came to increase the knowledge of sin, but we are no longer under the law but under the grace of God.

always dealing with two opposing forces. (See also Romans 7:18-19, 22-24. for more insights on this subject.).

In v.18 of Galatians 5, the Apostle Paul delivers the good news that if we are led by the Spirit, we are no longer subject to the penalty of the law. In Romans 8: 1, the Scripture tells us that *"There is therefore now no condemnation to them which are in Christ Jesus, who walk not after the flesh, but after the Spirit"*. Further in v.14 of this same Scripture we are told that *"For as many as are led by the Spirit of God, they are the sons of God"*; meaning that all our sins have been paid for with the precious blood of Jesus Christ, who gave His life a ransom for many (or for us).

In vv. 19-21, the chief Apostle, Saint Paul outlined a long list of all the sins that can be easily seen, and which a born again Christian must avoid. These are what the flesh lusted after, and which the Spirit is constantly against, and these two have been, and will always be in disagreement with one another. In vv. 22 and 23, we read of the nine fruit of the Holy Spirit, which are meant to preserve and prevent us from getting involved in the sins outlined in the last three verses of Galatians 5 (vv. 19-21).

The last three verses (vv.24-26) of Galatians 5, provides a summary of what we have read and heard so far on the subject of walking in the Spirit. As born again Christians and True Believers, in order for us to bear fruits and remain attached to the True Vine (Jesus), we must continue to walk in the Spirit and not in the flesh. We have already been given the gift of the Holy Spirit. Let us therefore walk in the Spirit, exercising the gift of God in each and every one of us, exercising the authority that God has vested in us, and taking dominion over all principalities and powers.

As born again Christians who walk in the Spirit, we should never forget that though we are in the world that we are not of the world. Galatians 5:24 says: *And they that are Christ's have crucified the flesh with the affections and lusts"*, and vv. 25-26 cautions us and state thus: **"If we live in the Spirit, let us also walk in the Spirit. Let us not be desirous of vain glory, provoking one another, envying one another".**

In Romans 6:12-14, Apostle Paul also admonishes the believers in Rome and clearly said thus: "Let not sin therefore reign in your mortal body, that you should obey it in the lusts thereof. Neither yield you your members as instruments of unrighteousness to sin; but yield yourselves to God, as those that are alive from the dead, and your members as instruments of righteousness to God. Sin shall not have dominion over you; for you are not under law, but under grace".

May God help us to cease to function as live wires and circuit breakers for Satan. Instead, let us continue to live as God's workmanship and vessels, and as the salt of the earth and light of the world. We must cease to be advocates and agents of Satan in all our ways. While you have the Light, walk in the Light. In Jn. 3:3 Jesus said, *"Verily, verily I say unto thee, Except a man be born again, he cannot see the Kingdom of God".* We must be born of the Spirit in order for us to inherit the Kingdom of God. In 1 Peter 2:9, the Apostle Peter writes to remind us that we are *"a chosen generation, a royal priesthood, an holy nation, a peculiar people; that ye* *should show forth the praises of him who hath called you out of darkness into his marvelous light".*

In vv.21-23 of the first chapter of his letter to the Church in Colossi (Colossians 1:21-23), the Apostle Paul reminds us that even though we were people who were once lost in our minds and became strangers by sinful works, God still accepted us and made us princes and princesses, and that we have redemption and are reconciled to God. Beginning from v.21 of this Scripture, Apostle Paul writes: *"And you, who once were alienated and enemies in your mind by wicked works, yet now He has reconciled in the body of His flesh through death, to present you holy, and blameless, and above reproach in His sight, if indeed you continue in the faith, grounded and steadfast, and are not moved away from the hope of the gospel which you heard, which was preached to every creature under heaven, of which Paul I became a minister".*

In other words, we have received full assurance that if we steadfastly remain faithful until Christ returns, He will present us holy and blameless before His Father. In Chapter 12 and verse 2 of his letter to the Church in Rome, the Apostle Paul advises as follows: "And do not be conformed to this world, but be transformed by the renewing of your mind, that you may prove what is that good and acceptable and perfect will of God".

To know more on this topic of Walking in the Spirit, we may also go to the following, related Scripture references: Acts 2: 37-38, 43, John 14: 17, Romans

8:9, 1 Cor. 3:16, 6:19, II Timothy 1:14, 1 John 2:27, Joel 2:28, and John 15:5-7, 16.

Other Names Used in The Bible To Qualify The Holy Spirit otherwise referred to as the Spirit (with an uppercase alphabet, "S") can be found in what are known as "The 6's, 7's and 8's of The Holy Spirit", and have been so named because each referenced Scripture contains either the number 6, 7, or 8.

In Jn. 14:16, He is called The Abiding Guest, The Comforter.

In Jn. 14:26, He is referred to as The Teacher and Remembrancer.

In Jn. 15:26, the Scripture addresses Him as The Testifier.

Jn. 16:8-7 called Him The Reprover.

Jn. 16:13, declares Him as The Guide, The Voice of God, The Prophet.

In Jn. 16:14, the Scripture introduces Him as The Glorifier of Jesus.

He is known in Jn. 16:15 as The Exhibitor of Jesus.

Acts 1:8 addresses the Holy Spirit as The Spiritual Dynamo.

In Rm. 8:16, He is The Witness of Sonship.

Rm. 8:16, says that He is The Helper in Prayer.

Finally, in Rev. 22: 17 we are privileged to read that He is The Solicitor and The Chief Advocate.

Now, knowing that we have this divine relationship with Him, we must refrain and indeed cease from indulging in the habit of "eye service" as with men pleasers but instead, we must adopt the spirit of obedience, loyalty and faithfulness to God and steadfastly walking in the spirit, knowing that he who sees our hearts and knows us even before we were formed in our mothers' wombs, is omniscient. If we are not serving and loving God in the way we did when we were first saved, then we must have backslidden somewhere along the line. We must therefore, ask God for forgiveness, while renewing our covenant with Him and adopting the 'Ministry of Mary Magdalene' and decide wholeheartedly to sin no more.

We must return to our right minds, appreciate what our Heavenly Father has for us and come back home as the prodigal son did. We must shine and radiate in the anointing and glory of the Lord. We must let the world see God in us when we talk, let them see Him when we walk, let them see Him in the way we dress, let them feel Him when we sing, let them see Him when we teach, and let them see Him when we preach. Let the world see Him in all aspects of our life. Let your light so shine, so that the world may see God in you and glorify Him. We are a chosen generation created to show God's excellence. We need to "die daily" with Jesus, and our lives must be profitable for the Kingdom of God; it must bring light and increase to the world. Let's not lose our vision for our passion. We must learn to live as peace-makers and not as woe mongers.

As we end this chapter, I feel obligated to share this testimony of personal experience with demonic attack; hence, the Scriptures tell us that we overcome by the Blood of the Lamb and by the words of our testimonies. On Sunday July 14, 2013, during an evening service at my home Church in New York City, a call for healing prayers was made specifically for three brethren in the Sanctuary by the Pastor in charge of that very service as the Holy Spirit directed him. The Pastor also asked another pastor and I to assist him with the prayer, as we joined our hearts together in one accord and in the Spirit to pray for the afflicted brethren.

As we prayed, and as the strength of the prayers intensified, one of the brethren we were praying for fell at the altar and immediately, my entire body felt so squeezed and as though there were two strong men tying me up with ropes, with one pulling one end and the other pulling the other end. At that point I felt an excruciating pain, suffocation and an increased body heat together with heavy sweating; I indeed was losing my breath at that point. Meanwhile, while my brethren continued to pray for those who were called out, and with no knowledge of my situation, all I was doing was to continue shouting "name of Jesus, Blood of Jesus".

One may ask, but why did he continue to shout those words instead of saying the normal prayer? I did so because the two things the devil fears terribly are the name of Jesus and the Blood of Jesus. Hence, at the mention of Jesus, every knee must bow and every tongue must confess that Jesus is Lord. We are indeed redeemed by the shedding of the Blood of Jesus (the Blood of the Lamb of God) on the Cross of Calvary.

Modern medicine was not the solution to my situation and could not help me at that time as doctors observed my painful condition, with a blood pressure of 160/80 but could not identify the cause of my pain. This was after several diagnostic and laboratory tests were performed, and test results obtained, and after spending a whole day at the emergency unit of the hospital.

A month later, on August 15, 2013, to be specific, a visiting prophet of God confirmed that I was demonically attacked on that day but that God intervened immediately the attack came, and which is what kept me alive after that attack. He (the prophet) then added that I have a pure and clean heart, and that I should never cease to love and serve the same God that I have been serving for He knows and cares for me. He prayed with me and finally left me with a spiritual prescription (including the specific line of prayers, the specific time, and the duration in terms of the number of days) that would take me to full recovery and I did exactly as he instructed me, without questions and doubts as Naaman did with Prophet Elisha. Indeed, my health was fully restored before my "spiritual prescription" could run out (and it will never run out as will be yours in Jesus name). Today, I am physically and spiritually stronger than ever. People of faith must walk by faith and not by sight, and should never question or doubt God when He speaks to us through His prophets.

We must therefore remain obedient, faithful and steadfast in our labor of love, as the called and the chosen ones, and as we humble ourselves in fasting and praying without ceasing.

When Elisha instructed Naaman the leper (2 Kings 5) to go and wash himself seven times in River Jordan so that he would be cleansed of his leprosy and his flesh restored, he responded with arrogance and anger out of ego. For those who are not familiar with *this Bible story, the Scripture states as follows in vv.11 and 12 of 2 Kings Chapter 5: "But Naaman was wroth and went away, and said, Behold, I thought, he will surely come out to me, and stand, and call on the name of the Lord his God, and strike his hand over the place, and recover the Leper. Are not Abana and Pharpar, rivers of Damascus, better than all the waters of Israel? May I not wash in them, and be clean? So he turned and went away in rage".*

We must therefore remain obedient, faithful and steadfast in our labor of love, as the called and the chosen ones, and as we humble ourselves in fasting and praying without ceasing. We must not cease to love the Lord our God with all our heart and with all our soul and with all our strength, and to have no other god besides Him as He requires from us in the first of His Ten Commandments. It is imperative that we seek, and remain in His presence every moment of our lives; living for Him like there is no tomorrow. Let's learn to access dominion by stewardship instead of verbalizing it without action and for vain glory.

We pray that we grow to be spiritually matured to the point that our mortal body be clothed by the power of God, so that we will be led by His Spirit, and be a revelation to our neighbors and our communities. We must move from Times Square to Jesus Square, from Trafalgar Square to the King of kings Square and most importantly, we must be spiritually transformed from being a mere "Daraprim Christian" to a complete, True Believer.

CHAPTER 6

Fasting And Biblical Counseling

Introduction

We introduce this chapter by, first and foremost, asking the question, "What is counseling?" The word "Counselor" derives from the Greek word "Paraklesis" meaning "to come alongside to encourage". In general, to counsel means to give advice or guidance on conduct and behavior or to wisely address certain issues and circumstances as they arise. In other words, counseling involves the flow of words of wisdom and prudence from one person (the counselor or adviser) to another (the counselee). It is concerned with guiding an individual with any form of psychological/emotional problem(s) such as depression towards the path of recovery, restoration and sanity.

It then means that a counselor must be a person of wisdom and of good character, who can reason not only constructively and objectively, but also responsibly. Such individual must also be a good listener, and, at the same time, be professionally trained and equipped to perform the duties of a counselor, including knowing all the dos and don'ts that are associated with the profession. This is where the need for fasting and prayers becomes imperative for the Christian Counselor or the Christocratic Adviser.

The Christian Counselor And The Secular Counselor

First and foremost, it is important to understand that some or most secular counselors are obscurants. An obscurant is an anti-religion person, who will certainly exclude elements of spirituality in his/her counseling sessions. Unlike the secular counselor, the Biblical counselor must be someone who has the ability to evangelize while providing advice to the counselee. He/she must be prepared to incorporate prayers and spirituality in all the counseling sessions. Christian Counseling must be aligned with the word of God.

Whereas some or most secular counselors believe in the science of evolution, the Christian Counselor believes that all things are created by God and that all wisdom and authority come from Him and from Him alone. They understand that He is the Creator King and the Master Architect, the Master Designer and the Master Builder. He is the Omniscience God, the Immortal, the Invisible and the only wise God. All divine power and authority come from Him.

The Christian Counselor must be Christocratic in all his/her practices. In other words, he/she must completely commit his/her life wholly and heartedly to the rulership and governance of the Kingdom of God, bearing in mind that they have the Kingdom Authority as Ambassadors of the Kingdom of the Most High. However, we must recognize that not all who call themselves Christians are True Believers but all True Believers, by definition, are Christians. Unlike the secular counselor, the Christian Counselor must understand that God's Counsel is supreme and irreplaceable. He/she knows that allowing the Holy Spirit to take absolute control in everything we do guarantees us positive and real results.

Realistically, we consciously believe that Biblical Counseling must adapt any approach that integrates Theology and Psychology. Hence, there is need for some elements of spirituality as well as some scientific evidences or empirical results in counseling. This therefore makes the Integrationist Approach more preferable to other Schools of Thought in Counseling and Psychology. The combination of psychological laws, rules and regulations, and the Bible gives the Christian Counselor an edge over secular counselors, who themselves are very humanistic in their approaches.

In the process of counseling, the counselor should study the counselee's communication patterns in terms of body language and non-verbal forms of communication and his/her verbal communication (including tone of voice, facial expressions, gestures, etc). The counselor should be able to incorporate prayer and the Scripture in his/her counseling sessions.

Biblical Counselors should use both scientific experiments and God's word, and indeed believe that the Word of God takes precedence over every other thing else. Some effective approaches such as the Extinction Procedure which involves the elimination of enforcing a behavior, for example, giving a child some candy when he is acting up in order to pacify him or her. The Extinction Procedure should not be stopped prematurely, nevertheless. It must be kept long enough to ensure a complete solution to

Biblical Counselors should use both scientific experiments and God's word, and indeed believe that the Word of God takes precedence over every other thing else.

the problem as presented. This is one of the simplest procedures, and it could be applied to for instance, cases of Developmental Disorder (DD) and Psychiatric Disorder (PD).

Biblical Counseling should be more than just a catchy word, phrase or cliché. Rather, it is a commitment to the Word of God with sincerity and with all seriousness to help in spreading the Gospel of Jesus Christ. As Biblical Counselors, we should also consider ourselves to be soul winners, and as we carry out the Great Commission of 'Go ye therefore and teach all nations, baptizing them in the name of the Father, and of the Son, and of the Holy Ghost:

Teaching them to Observe all things whatsoever I have commanded you: and lo, I am with you alway, even unto the end of the world' (Matt. 28:19-20).

The counselor could for instance tell the counselee a thought provoking message such as when God tries to deal with us and we keep doing things our own way. He allows things to happen to us that can be very traumatic so as to get our attention such as in the case of Jonah, when he found himself in the belly of a fish (Jonah 1-2:1). The counselee should be advised that as long as we live here on earth, that there will be trials and tribulations, and that God has promised us that He will deliver us from all afflictions, as long as we remain committed and connected to His priority, plan and purpose.

Sometimes, trials can be God's channels or avenues through which we triumph. He can make our problems become our promotion and our

Sometimes, trials can be God's channels or avenues through which we triumph.

obstacles become our stepping stone, springboard or ladder, which God uses to take us to our destiny or highest level even before we know it. According to Marvin Williams (William, Marvin, Our Daily Bread, January 2014), "when we are being tried in a crucible of distress, God desires to help us continue living by faith and trusting in His compassion and mercy".

Some evangelical Scripture references on Biblical Counseling which the Christian Counselor could cite during counseling sessions include but are not limited to the following:

- ➤ Psalm 16:7 – "I will bless the Lord who has counseled me."
- ➤ Psalm 73:24 – "With Thy Counsel, Thou will guide me".
- ➤ Isaiah 9:6 – "His name will be called Wonderful Counselor."
- ➤ Romans 15:4 – "Through the encouragement of Scriptures, we might have hope".
- ➤ Philippians 4:13 – "I can do all things through Christ which strengtheneth me".
- ➤ James 5:11 – "Indeed we count them blessed who endure. You have heard of the perseverance of Job and seen the end intended by the Lord; that the Lord is very compassionate and merciful."

If these are not enough references, then think of King David as detailed in the First and Second Books of Samuel in the Bible. As these Bible portions reveal to us, before King David decides to go and fight his enemies, he enquires from the Great and Wonderful Counselor (The Counsel General or the Supreme Councilor), the Great Jehovah, the Almighty God whether or not he should go. If God says "go, for I will deliver your enemies to you", he goes. Otherwise he would not. The Biblical Counselor should endeavor to make the Word work when dealing with those who are hurting and struggling with certain situations and circumstances which are beyond their comprehension. We must understand that people in need of counseling are looking for hope that are solutions to their hurts, their predicaments, and all the challenges they encounter each day

Certain approaches to counseling such as Correctional Study, has been effectively used prayerfully in Biblical Counseling. Theologically speaking, it is believed that prayer changes things, and based on this principle, the stronger the prayer, the greater the changes. A combination of fasting and prayers remains the greatest weapon we must use to combat the common enemy and adversary, Satan and all his agents.

Biblical counseling should always be started and ended with prayers as our Lord and Savior Jesus Christ did.

Biblical counseling should always be started and ended with prayers as our Lord and Savior Jesus Christ did. This does not mean that we should ignore the scientific aspects of counseling since the integration of both will often yield a better result. If we consider the case of depression which biblically and spiritually speaking demands living by faith and not by sight, we become more aligned to spirituality than to anything else. Counseling that is based on the Scripture is becoming very common at medical and health centers, and at correctional and psychiatric facilities, to mention but a few.

In the United States, however, that section of the Constitution which provided for the separation of

Church and State prevents the practice of Biblical Counseling within public educational environments, ranging from the primary and secondary schools to tertiary/higher institutions. To this effect, Christian Counselors are therefore incapacitated to biblically counsel within these environments due to this obstructive piece of legislation. When you observe obvious signs of lack of self-worth (worthlessness), low self-esteem and hopelessness in someone and you know what to do but you are restricted and legally incapacitated from doing so, you somehow start to develop some disappointment over the physical and political environment where you are at that particular time. I personally have been in that very situation, and, in fact, the world we live in is very humanistic in its approach to situations.

One of the most common areas of counseling is depression and many have taken their own lives as a result of this psychological and mental condition which tends to drain people of their feelings of self-worth, self-esteem, and hope. A recent case of interest is that of a Baptist Church Pastor in Atlanta, Georgia, USA who committed suicide because he believed that he had waited for too long for God to answer his prayers but He (God) did not (Welch, Edward, Light of The World, Vol. 11, No. 132, December 2013, p. 8). He therefore took his own life outside of his home (in his drive way to be specific) while his congregation, including his wife and children waited in anticipation of his arrival for the morning worship on a Sunday. He was scheduled to preach the Sermon (the Word) that very morning.

According to the source (Light of the World), this young Pastor (34 years young) battled manic depression, struggled to keep it secret, went through physical and emotional challenges before losing faith and finally terminated his own life. Although he was a strong preacher (who even preached against this "terminal" action he took), he struggled with depression for many years and by keeping the problem secret, it became even more difficult for him to get the help he obviously needed while he still lived.

Suicide, which is often the brain child of depression, is impossible to predict and most often, the person we least expected to commit suicide is the one that will do it. This means that we need to love wisely and relate to one another kindly and affectionately as long as we live. As the Scripture teaches us, love is the most excellent way. Though we may try to do goodwill to others and do whatever we believe is right, if we do not have love the Scripture tells us that we are like sounding cymbals or empty vessels and it profits us nothing. If we show more love and affection to others, both relatives and non-relatives, we may make positive impact in the lives of those around us. The Christian Counselor must understand that he/she is the salt of the earth and the light of the world and should therefore function accordingly while performing the work of a Counselor.

For the depressed persons, most of the time loneliness is not the absence of affection but the absence of direction. When anxiety takes the place of confidence and the spirit of fear displaces the spirit of sound mind in people's lives, they automatically ignore what the Scripture tells us in Philippians 4[:13, 19], 2 Corinthians 10[: 4-5], and many more. These portions of the Word of God are meant to comfort the hopeless, the mentally exhausted, the afflicted, and the weary and heavily burdened. Christian Counselees or those who are depressed should remember in times like this that they have been given the key to the Kingdom to bind and to loose. Therefore, He that is in them and in each believer is greater than he that is in world, and that anointing breaks every yoke and every chain.

Most often, it is the lack of endurance as well as not exercising longsuffering that make individuals resort to unimaginable actions in their lives including taking their precious lives. The depressed persons must be informed that what doesn't kill them will make them stronger, and that those that endure to the end shall inherit the earth.

A Summary

Overall, we should understand that people in need of counseling, otherwise known as counselees, are looking for hope that there are solutions to their hurts, predicaments and all the challenges they encounter on a daily basis. Therefore, the Biblical Counselor should endeavor to make the Word of God work when dealing with individuals who are going through some difficult period at any particular moment in their lives.

The Biblical Counselor must always equip himself/ herself with the Sword of the Spirit, which is the Word of God, while also observing fasts, and praying without ceasing. Counselees should be advised so as to comprehend that the peace available to us in God quiets us in a way that the world does not understand or embrace. They should understand, and tap into the incredible spiritual relief and calmness that songs, hymns and melodies provide from the challenges each one of us face day by day. David played his musical instrument (harp) and sang melodies to King Saul to serenade and help him regain his sanity whenever he became mentally, spiritually and emotionally unstable, as the evil spirit sent from God came upon him. In the Book of 1 Samuel 16:23, the Scripture says as follows:

The Biblical Counselor must always equip himself/herself with the Sword of the Spirit, which is the Word of God, while also observing fasts, and praying without ceasing.

"And it came to pass when the evil spirit from God was upon Saul, that David took the harp, and played with his hand: so Saul was refreshed, and was well, and the evil spirit departed from him". We must therefore not forget to utilize the rejuvenating power of heavenly music in our moments of emotional weakness and spiritual stagnation.

With Biblical Counseling, the Counselor is enabled to behave differently by dependence upon our Lord Jesus Christ (Colossians 1:27) Particularly the Biblical

Counselor should make every effort to listen and understand those who are hurting and struggling with situations/circumstances that are beyond their comprehension. Biblical Counsel can serve evangelistic purpose as expressed on the Day of the Pentecost (Acts 2), and as in the case of The Great Commission (Matt. 28:19-20). The Counselor must avoid over-reaction of aversion to psychology, while remaining professional and focused.

Counselees, particularly the unbelievers, would most often insist on seeing some tangible outcomes or facts from prior counseling of some other individuals with similar problem(s). They will often demand to see empirical evidences in order to be convinced of what the counselor is saying. In other words, counselees need evidences beyond faith and spirituality, and this represents one of the key differences between Biblical Counseling and counseling in the secular, humanistic world. This then is where the Integrationist Approach to counseling and psychology comes into play, and in which we combine Theology/Spirituality and psychology, while making references to past scientific experiments and results.

counseling must be a selfless endeavor embedded in love, and the Christian Counselor should always remember that within True Discipleship love is contagious and it begins with the Christian Counselor, and with every True Believer.

In sum, counseling must be a selfless endeavor embedded in love, and the Christian Counselor should always remember that within True Discipleship love is contagious and it begins with the Christian Counselor, and with every True Believer. Biblical Counseling must be Christ-centered, nevertheless. Ultimately, spirituality takes precedence over scientific studies and experiments since God is, and will always be the Author and Finisher of our faith. Remember that when all else fails us, God shows up to heal our broken hearts for He is the Master Counselor. The Christian Counselor should always remember that the objective of counseling is to guide the depressed, the hopeless, the broken-hearted, or persons with any form of psychological/emotional problem(s) towards the path of recovery, restoration and sanity. Once he/she has that kind of mindset, it will then become easier and less burdensome to accomplish the goal of Biblical Counseling.

When we fail to fast and pray before we counsel others, we may end up with the "counsel of Ahithophel" instead of applying the wisdom of God. It is very imperative that the Biblical Counselor know that although we need both knowledge and wisdom when counseling, there is a difference between the two. Whereas knowledge is the awareness or familiarity gained by experience or learning, wisdom is the appropriate application of knowledge or intelligence at the right time. In other words, in as much as we know something, we need to seek the divine wisdom that comes from God in order to rightly apply it.

CHAPTER 7

Let Go And Let God

Let go, and let God take over and fix whatever you're not able, and may never be able to fix in your life, for He has said that the battle is not yours but His, and has promised that He will fight all your battles for you. We must cease to live a bitter life by letting go our regrets of yesteryears, and unloading the negative luggage of yesterday. Sometimes, it becomes the case of "love thyself as thy neighbor"; instead of "love thy neighbor as thyself".

Let go, and let God take over and fix whatever you're not able, and may never be able to fix in your life.

I am yet to meet a normal human being who has no regrets of the way they handled some issues or of why they did what they did in the past. As the Scripture tells us, all we like sheep have gone astray. We must not dwell in the regrets of the past and continue to live a sympathetic life that weighs us down. We must learn to forgive our own selves so we can be able to forgive others. Charity begins at home. Therefore you should begin your forgiveness journey from yourself and then extend it to your offenders and accusers. In fact, we must see the act of forgiveness as something contagious and which must begin with each one of us and then radiate to those who trespassed against us.

Dwelling on the regrets of the past and tagging along the heaviness of the negative loads of yesterday will block our blessings and breakthroughs of tomorrow. We must endeavor to have a pure, clean and uncluttered heart in order for us to reap the full benefits of the blessings of God. Also, we must never forget that our bodies are the living temples of God and therefore, should be rid of all filthiness, including anger and hatred. We must let go, and let God.

Some people may possibly have developed some kinds of cardiac illnesses by being so bitter with their lives, and many bitter individuals tend to be chronic gossipers and lovers of heresies. They tend to be full of envy and hate, and often will try to verbally destroy other persons in their desperate attempts to seek sympathy. Some of us carry more than a ship load of negative issues and bitterness to the extent that it radiates and pollutes their social environment.

Let's not continue to dwell in the past; we must let go of things we cannot be able to reverse or change and allow God to take over our circumstances for He is omniscient, and faithful to all those who call upon His

Holy Name. God said that He will fight our battles for us. You may recall how the battle between the children of Israel and the joint forces of the Ammonites, the Moabites, and the children of mount Seir ended as chronicled in 2 Chronicles Chapter 20. Did the children of Israel fight in that battle? No, they did not, but God fought for them in that, and in many other battles.

One of the most painful feelings we sometimes experience in our lifetime comes when we are falsely accused for something we did not say or did not do, or when we are humiliated and embarrassed publicly. In fact the most painful part of such accusations comes when we try to swallow our ego and guts to resist the temptation of retaliation and unforgiveness. Many Christians have suffered this type of persecution even as the devil decides to use one person against another as his agent. And still harder to do is to forget an incident or event after you must have forgiven the one who the devil used to destroy your personality and assassinate your character. But as True Believers, we must endeavor to forgive and forget, and no matter how hard, or how painful that could be. Let's not count the cost of forgiveness before doing the act, for if we take that route, we may never forgive.

One of the most painful feelings we sometimes experience in our lifetime comes when we are falsely accused for something we did not say or did not do, or when we are humiliated and embarrassed publicly.

Nevertheless, in Matthew 18:21-22, the Scripture tells us that the Apostle Peter came and asked Jesus and said, *"Lord, how oft shall my brother sin against me, and I forgive him? Till seven times? Jesus saith unto him, I say not unto thee, Until seven times: but, Until seventy times seven"*. In fact, the words of Jesus on the topic of forgiveness as recorded in the Gospel according to St. Luke (Luke 17:3-4) are noteworthy to each and every one of us. In that Scripture, Jesus said to His disciples: *"Take heed to yourselves: If thy brother trespass against thee, rebuke him; and if he repent, forgive him. And if he trespasses against thee seven times in a day, and seven times in a day turn again to thee, saying, I repent, thou shall forgive him"*. Taking a step back in Luke 17:1-2, Jesus also said these words to His disciples regarding offenses and those through which they come: *"It is impossible but that offenses come: but woe unto him, through whom they come! It were better for him that a millstone were hanged about his neck, and he cast into the sea, than that he should offend one of these little ones"*.

We must therefore cease from provoking one another, knowing that there are grievous consequences of such action. In Ephesians 4:25, Apostle Paul warns the Body of Christ at Ephesus saying: "Therefore each of you must put off falsehood and speak truthfully to your neighbor, for we are all members of one body". Let's endeavor to speak graciously to one another using words that edify, encourage and uplift the spirit of those around us. Are you one of those individuals who keep a diary of the wrongs others did to them?

If so, it is time for you to shred it and thereby replace hatred and unforgiveness with love and forgiveness. Ephesians 4:31 tells us to "Get rid of all bitterness, rage and anger, brawling and slander, along with every form of malice". We must indeed develop the spirit of forgiving one another, since we have been given the spirit of reconciliation. Remember that we always pray to God, asking Him to "forgive us our trespasses as we forgive those who trespass against us". But we often forget the second part of this very prayer when we are dealing with those who trespassed against us.

Notwithstanding, forgiving and forgetting is a major aspect of Christian maturity, and it is Christ-like, indeed, to do so. Be it known to each and every one of us that the spirit of unforgiveness is a very cancerous one, and therefore those who decide in their heart not to forgive those who wronged or did evil thing(s) to them should beware of the danger they face. The Scriptures makes it clear to us in 1 Jn. 3:15 that: ***"Whosoever hated his brother is a murderer: and ye know that no murderer hath eternal life abiding in him".***

Furthermore, the Scripture says: *"As much as is possible, be at peace with all men".* The sin of unforgiveness can indeed destroy a man or woman; it is very cancerous by itself, but within the Body of Christ (the household of faith), love is contagious, and it must begin with us. Letting go and letting God means that we should cease from practicing what the author refers to as discriminatory, fenced, or selective love in which we pick and choose who to love and who to hate, and which has been found to exist even within the Church family. This behavior is even more pronounced among the "holier than thou" individuals within the Body of Christ and who, in most instances, display their acts in such a way that it becomes very obvious. (They find it very difficult to hide their feelings which becomes so obviously expressed in their countenances.) We must persevere, and cease not to intercede for such individuals.

You may have noticed sometimes when a man or woman of God is either preaching or conducting a service and an individual or individuals will get up from their seat in the Sanctuary and walk away with a frowning or disgusting face as a sign of their disapproval of the one God is using to deliver His message to His people. Sometimes our countenance (facial expression or mood) changes immediately a fellow believer walks in where we are or walks by us, and which signifies how we view or value that brother or sister. At any level of spirituality we may be, if we find it difficult to cordially relate to everyone within the household of faith as family members, then we have a big problem. We need to repent, indeed, and ask God for forgiveness; for all we like sheep have gone astray. We must let go the spirit of "holier than thou", and hatred but instead, replace it with agape love towards one another. The Scripture in 1 John 1$^{:8-10}$ says that: *If we say we have no sin we deceive ourselves, and the truth is not in us. If we confess our sins, He is faithful and just to forgive us our sins and to cleanse us from all unrighteousness. If we say that we have not sinned, we make Him a liar, and the Word is not in us.*

If we are all "Mr. Perfects" and "Ms. Perfects", why then was Christ crucified? We must first of all take away the logs in our own eyes before we can see the specks in our neighbor's eyes. Think of the case of Mary Magdalene and the mobs of Pharisees, who accused her of the sin of adultery and were determined to stone her to death before she ran to Jesus (the Rock of our Salvation) and He intervened, and saved her. We must ask the Holy Spirit to take absolute control of our lives, and to remove the veil that is covering our spiritual face, so we may spiritually see beyond what we are unable to see on our own.

If we are all "Mr. Perfects" and "Ms. Perfects", why then was Christ crucified?

The Apostle Peter, in Chapter 3 of his First Epistle General (1 Peter 3), wrote to members of the Body of Christ who were suffering persecution while they were scattered in what we know as the present day Turkey regarding love and forgiveness. Particularly in vv. 8-9, he said to the Church: *"Finally, be ye all of one mind, having compassion one of another, love as brethren, be pitiful, be courteous: Not rendering evil for evil, or railing for railing; but contrariwise blessing; knowing that ye are thereunto called, that ye should inherit a blessing".*

Remember what Jesus taught us in the Sermon on the Mount (also known as The Beatitudes) as recorded in the Gospel according to Saint Matthew from Chapter 5:3 through Chapter 7:27. Every word that proceeded out of Jesus' mouth in that powerful sermon is important to each and every one of us and we must endeavor to read every single word from that Scripture as it is written. Particularly relating to the matter of forgiving one another, the King of kings in Matthew 7:1-3 cautioned us about judging one another, and said: *"Judge not, that ye be not judged. For with what judgment ye judge, ye shall be judged: and with what measure ye mete, it shall be measured to you again. And why beholdest thou the mote that is in your brother's eye, but considerest not the beam that is in thine own eye".*

The First General Epistle of Apostle John, 1 John 2:9-11 talks about hatred, false profession, spiritual darkness, and brotherly love. In v.9, the Apostle cautions and states that *"He that saith that he is in the light, and hated his brother is in darkness even till now".* He then continued in vv.10-11 and said *"He that loveth his brother abideth in the light, and there is no occasion of stumbling in him. But he that hateth his brother is in darkness, and knoweth not whither he goeth because the darkness has blinded his eyes".* Evidently, the focus of the first four chapters of 1 John is on brotherly love and the difference between True Believers and the unbelievers. Specifically, v.10 of Chapter 3 says that *"In this, the children of God are manifest, and the children of devil: whosoever doeth not righteousness is not of God, neither he that loveth not his brother".*

As for those who avail themselves for the work of the devil, provoking their brethren and neighbors, read again what our King and Master, Jesus taught us in the Sermon on the Mount in Matt. 7:12, whereby He said *"Therefore, all things whatsoever you would that men should do to you, even so do to them: for this is the law and the prophets"*. In a very simple language, what Jesus said is that we should treat other persons as we would expect them to treat us. This means that we must respect one another, and respect in itself is a very mutual thing indeed. Mutually respecting and understanding one another is the key to a peaceful co-existence which, of course, is what our society desperately needs and which in turn, symbolizes Jesus.

Notwithstanding, some ordained servants of God in many churches today indulge in this so ungodly and hypocritical behavior by being very nice and rosy to some members of their congregation, but extremely hateful and unfriendly to many others. This indeed is not Christ-like; it ought not to be so and therefore, those who unfortunately belong to such infamous group of individuals must repent from it and instead, start practicing unconditional, unfenced, non-selective, and non-discriminatory type of love, which by itself, comes peaceably.

This makes one sometimes to wonder if such ordained ministers and shepherds are truly real men and women of God who have actually been called to serve and/ or to lead the flock. As people created in God's very own image, we must learn to love one another even as Christ loved the Church. This means that we must rid our hearts of all malice, hate and filthiness, and instead refill and permanently replace them with love, affection, friendliness and care for one another. The Scriptures tell us to love one another and so to fulfill the law of Christ.

Within the Body of Christ (as stated earlier in this text), we can boldly say that love is contagious, and it begins with you and I. In the fourth Chapter of his first Epistle (1 John 4), the Apostle John devoted so much of his time to teach us about this word called love and why it is imperative that each and every one of us should endeavor to practice it daily, and make it a part of our lives. Hebrews 10:24 reminds us that we should endeavor to uplift (edify) one another's spirit rather than belittling and demoralizing our fellow brothers and sisters, which indeed is not of God. Specifically, that Scripture says: *"Let us consider how we may spur one another on toward love and good deeds"*. Let us be "path finders", rather than "fault finders" towards our fellow human beings. We must learn to *"comfort each other and edify one another"* as the Scripture tells us in 1 Thessalonians 5:11. We must cease to hate, envy or jealous one another.

As True Believers or practicing Christians, we must not forget that we have been called to season the earth and to show light to those who are in darkness as the Salt of the Earth and Light of the World. Therefore, let your light so shine so that the world may see Christ in you and draw near to Him. Stay away from gossiping and heresies for these are demonic, and the devil uses such things to create enmity and division between us so as to weaken and conquer us. In I Peter 3:8-11 Apostle Peter taught the Church about keeping good conscience. Beginning from v.8, the Apostle said: *"Finally, (my brethren),* **be you all of one mind, having compassion one for another, love as brethren, be pitiful, be courteous: Not rendering evil for evil, or railing for railing; but contrariwise blessing,** *knowing that you are thereunto called, that you should inherit a blessing. For he will love life and see good days,* **let him refrain his tongue from evil, and his lips that they speak no guile: Let him eschew evil, and do good; let him seek peace and ensue it"**.

Oftentimes we tend to hate one another out of jealousy and envy, but at the same time we become ignorant of the fact that God is the one that gives us the talent according to each one's ability. We see this in the Parable of Talents as told by Jesus in Matthew 25:14-30, and in the letter of the Apostle Paul to the Church in Ephesus as written in Ephesians 4:11 regarding the Five Fold Ministry. In the later Scripture, the Apostle Paul writes as follows: *"And he gave some, apostles; and some, prophets; and some, evangelists; and some pastors and teachers"*. In other words, not every one of us shall be a prophet or a pope for that matter. Neither will everyone be the president of a multinational, multimillion, corporation, nor be the president of a nation.

> *Oftentimes we tend to hate one another out of jealousy and envy, but at the same time we become ignorant of the fact that God is the one that gives us the talent according to each one's ability.*

At any point of time in this life, there will always be employers and employees, there will be landlords and tenants, teachers and students, the poor and the rich; there will be bishops and there will also be pastors, there will be prophets, and there will be apostles, with each one performing his/her functions according to the level of talent that God has given us. Just as the five fingers on our hands are not equal in size, so also are our talents; each one of us has a different talent and calling. In Romans 12:3-8, the Chief Apostle, Paul writes: *"For I say, through the grace given to me, to everyone who is among you, not to think of himself more highly than he ought to think, but to think soberly, as God has dealt to each one a measure of faith. For as we have many members in one body, but all the members do not have the same function, so we, being many, are one body in Christ, and individually members of one another. Having then gifts differing according to the grace that is given to us, let us use them; if prophecy, let us prophesy in proportion to our faith; or*

> *We must therefore refrain from unnecessarily hating and envying one another but instead, rejoice with those who are rejoicing and mourn with those who are mourning.*

ministry, let us use it in our ministering; he who teaches, in teaching; he who exhorts, in exhortation; he who gives, with liberality; he who leads, with diligence; he who shows mercy, with cheerfulness".

We must therefore refrain from unnecessarily hating and envying one another but instead, rejoice with those who are rejoicing and mourn with those who are mourning. Let's also not forget that no condition is permanent in this world; God may decide to change our situations and circumstances at any moment, as He pleases. Our lives are in His hands; He holds the key to our lives.

In all these, do not let the enemy use you as his agent to destroy your brother or your sister. In other words, as much as is possible, endeavor not to be an agent of Satan, nor be his recruit or advocate. Know this: When we intentionally and wrongfully accuse other persons for the crime they did not commit and thereby, tarnishing their image and damaging their reputation, we become twice as guilty as committing the crime ourselves. Let's not be quick in judging one another but instead, let us be wise to think and to reason prudently as God's children before we speak or act. When we speak before we think, we find ourselves later regretting what we shouldn't have said but already said it. It is ungodly to stereo-type other persons. Do not judge or relate to others based on what you heard about them from other persons. See for yourself before you conclude and do not let someone else cause you to commit the sin of hatred.

Remember that unity is strength, and that united we stand, divided we fall. Love thy neighbor as thyself, and as much as is possible, be at peace with all men, and be your brother's keeper. Don't be a Cain, who envied and hated his own brother so much to the point of taking his life, but be a Joseph, instead. Despite all the evils that his brothers did to him (including being extremely jealous and envious of him), and as he went from the pit to the prison and then to the palace, Joseph (one of the twelve sons of Jacob or Israel) still found some soft spots in his heart to embrace and love his brothers more, even as they were facing starvation and were in desperate need for food. Some of us could have ceased that opportunity to retaliate and "pay them back in their own coins".

In the case of Cain (one of the first two sons born on earth to the first parents, Adam and Eve), he slew his own brother, Abel because he (Cain) was so jealous and wroth after knowing that God has blessed and favored Abel, who offered a more pleasant and excellent sacrifice to Him. The Scripture, in vv.3-8 of Genesis Chapter 4, says that Abel offered a more pleasant and excellent sacrifice to God. Therefore God had respect for him and to his offering, and blessed him. Again, in Hebrews 11:4, the Scripture tells us that by faith Abel offered unto God a more excellent sacrifice and for that reason, God had more respect for him and to his offering, and blessed him. In v.9 of Genesis 4, Cain's response to God of *"Am I my brother's keeper?"*, when he was asked, *"Where is Abel thy brother?"* is a clear indication that he was still wroth and jealous over the fact that he did not give a worthy offering to God as his brother faithfully did, and therefore did not receive the approval and blessings of the Lord. But we must understand this simple spiritual fact that "there is no peace for the wicked" as it was in the case of Cain, the murderer.

Love covers a multitude of sins, does no harm to a neighbor: therefore, love is the fulfillment of the law (Romans 13:10). Since the Scriptures teach us that love covers a multitude of sins therefore, whom you love you would easily overlook whatever evil thing they have done to you. Jesus tells us in John 13:34-35 saying: "By this everyone will know that you are my disciples, if you love one another". When we speak of love, which is also called charity, we could see Chapter 13 of the first letter of Apostle Paul to the Corinthian Church as a "Love Letter", in which he gave the True Believer's definition of the word "love". The Scripture states in 1 Corinthians 13:2 that: "If I have the gift of prophecy and can fathom all mysteries and all knowledge, and if I have a faith that can move mountains, but do not have love, I am nothing". Truly, the distinguishing characteristic of a True Believer would be love, and that is the very reason why our Lord Jesus, the Christ made so much emphasis on it moments before He was crucified.

Love covers a multitude of sins, does no harm to a neighbor: therefore, love is the fulfillment of the law (Romans 13:10).

Given that we are constantly at war with God's arch enemy, Satan, it is imperative therefore, that we remain in the spirit of the upper room as it was in the day of the Pentecost; remaining in one accord and breaking bread together always. The Apostle Paul, while addressing the Church in Rome, said in Romans 13:12B-14: *"Therefore, let us cast off the works of darkness, and let us put on the armor of light. Let us walk properly, as in* the day, not in revelry and drunkenness, not in lewdness and lust, not in strife and envy. **But put on the Lord Jesus Christ, and make no provision for the flesh, to fulfill its lusts**". So, are you one of those individuals who are blocking their own blessings because they wouldn't forgive those who have offended or trespassed against them? By any and all means possible, endeavor not to destroy and bury your future and destiny because of unforgiving spirit that you wouldn't let go.

Unforgiveness, by itself, is a sin and we must ask God to grant us the spiritual strength and courage to forgive anyone who offends us. Remember what Jesus said on the cross as He was ridiculed, insulted, and assaulted by the Roman soldiers; 'Father forgive them for they do not know what they do". This means then that we must be bold enough and spiritually strong to bless those that curse us, and as much as it is possible on our parts, to be at peace with everyone.

In other words, as we continue to bless those who curse us, and deal kindly with those who continue to do evil things to us, we "heap coals of fire upon their heads".

We end this chapter with the following quotations from the Discovery Series pamphlet titled What Is True Forgiveness?, and written by Gary Inrig, (2006), RBC Ministries, Grand Rapids, Michigan: "Unforgiveness is deadly in more ways than one. We need to resist the temptation to keep those who sinned against us in an emotional penalty box, making them serve endless hard time for their offenses." In other words, as we continue to bless those who curse us, and deal kindly with those who continue to do evil things to us, we "heap coals of fire upon their heads".

True forgiveness, as Gary Inrig stated, begins by dealing with sin honestly. Many things may irritate, annoy, or upset us about someone else. He maintained that "those things may require enduring; they do not involve forgiving." Lastly (and according to Inrig), "forgiveness doesn't involve ignoring or denying sin, turning a blind eye to the misdeeds of another, or pretending it didn't happen". All in all, we must not forget that we cannot become a topic until we are at the top or until we have become successful. "Unachievers" are never a topic for gossiping. Instead, they are instruments for gossiping.

CHAPTER **8**

What We Have Learned

We often pray to God to grant us the wisdom to discern between good and evil, and He graciously gives us His divine gift of knowledge, wisdom and understanding (KWU). Knowledge is power, and more so, he who has divine knowledge will always be the head and not the tail. In the foregoing chapters, we have learned what it means to fast and pray as well as what it means to be a True Believer, we also received an understanding of the term "true religion".

In the introductory chapter, an overview of the power of fasting as experienced by men and women of God in the Bible was presented. In Chapter 2, we learned of the reason(s) why we should fast and pray, and make it a part of our daily living. The significance of fasting and prayer in the life of a Christian was clearly expressed with biblical examples including those of Abraham, Moses, Hannah, Joseph, Jabez, Daniel, King Jehoshaphat, to mention but a few.

In Chapter 3, we read about what the Church or who the Church is. We also learned what it means to be a True Believer and what true discipleship is all about. In Chapter 4, the Spiritual, physical and socio-economic benefits of fasting and prayer were revealed, including miracles, signs, wonders and various kinds of breakthroughs. Christians must learn how to walk with God, and crave for His divine presence always, just as the deer pants for the waters of the brooks. Covenanting with God and walking in the Spirit (the Holy Spirit) is very necessary. We learned how men and women of God who walked with God (as recorded in the Scriptures) were able to overcome all trials and tribulations they faced, including how God fought their numerous battles with their enemies. Both individual and communal requests were granted by God to those who obeyed Him and walked with Him, and as they put all their trust in Him.

As those who have been called to walk in God's vineyard and to take dominion on the earth, we must endeavor to be active participants and function as Biblical Counselors to those who are broken-hearted, hopeless and discouraged with life experiences. It is for this reason Chapter 6 dealt with Fasting and Biblical Counseling. The differences between psychology and Spirituality were revealed. We further learned that these two must work together in order to deal with the social and psychological problems that have continued to plague our society.

One of the major sins that is so common, and particularly among the Body of Christ and within biological families, is the sin of unforgiveness. This is a very troubling situation and it is for that reason that Chapter 7 wisely addressed the issue in Let Go, and Let God. We must cease to live bitter and vengeful lives by letting go the regrets of yesterday, and unloading the negative and heavy loads of yesteryears. In other

One of the major sins that is so common, and particularly among the Body of Christ and within biological families, is the sin of unforgiveness.

words, we must endeavor to first of all forgive and be at peace with our own selves and then be in the right state of mind, or be aligned with God to forgive those who trespassed against us, and love our neighbors as ourselves. It is only until we have done this that we can boldly come before God's presence and ask Him to "forgive us our trespasses as we forgive those who trespassed against us".

As we move forward in our life journeys, we must not cease to make fasting and prayer a part of our daily life. Know that a non-praying Christian is a "dead" Christian, and such a person will become more vulnerable to the attacks of the enemy and an easy prey to him. Watch and pray, therefore, for no one knows neither the day nor the hour when the Bridegroom (The Christ) shall return; and whether or not you believe it, He will surely return as He has promised us. In closing, one song that comes to mind, and which I recommend for everyone when fasting, goes as follows:

Put on the garments of praise for the spirit of heaviness,

Lift up your voice in praise!

Pray in the Spirit and with understanding,

O! Magnify the Lord

__Chorus:__

I will put on the garments of praise (2X)

For the spirit of heaviness, is gone from me

I will put on the garments of praise!

CHAPTER 9

Moving Forward

If you have not been fasting, I encourage you to start doing so today, and particularly, doing it with faith in God, and then watch and see the benefits of engaging in the habit of fasting and praying. When we fast and pray, we are binding the devil and all principalities and powers because we get ourselves in the mood of engaging the enemy and activating the power and authority that God has vested in each of us as His children and His representatives here on earth. When we cease to fast and pray, we make ourselves vulnerable to the attacks of the enemy and thereby become easy preys to him and his agents or cohorts.

You must know that to fast for several days is not an easy road to walk, but you can do it, for with God nothing shall be impossible to them that believe. As Saint Paul the great Apostle tells us in his letter to the

Philippians, Chapter 4 and vs. 13, *"We can do all things through Christ who strengthens us"*. You may start by skipping a meal a day and finding a quiet time to focus on God as you pray, meditate and sing melodies and praises to Him in your heart. It is imperative for us to first of all bind the spirit of distraction as we meditate and pray when we fast. This is to enable us remain focused and attentive as we draw nearer to God, and for us to hear Him and avoid missing what He has in store for us.

The truth about fasting is that God sees our hearts and intentions, and understands us as we engage in this spiritual practice. As the Scripture teaches us, we should know that in His presence that there is fullness of joy and His joy gives us strength. We also know that in His presence there is holiness and righteousness, and therefore those who come to Him must do so in spirit and in truth, and with reverence.

Fasting with ungodly or evil motives will not yield any positive result.

When we fast, it is not how many meals we miss in a day, in a week, or in a month that matters to God. In fact, when we skip meals without praying or meditating and making some time to have a quiet, intimate moment with God, then we are simply self-imposing starvation on ourselves. Skipping just one meal a day and engaging in serious prayers, praises and meditation for the entire day is more powerful and effective than skipping the entire day's meals without prayers and/or meditation. Fasting with ungodly or evil motives will not yield any positive result. Instead, it tends to lead the individual into more misery, frustrations, trials and tribulations.

In fact, if you are a part of a fasting and prayer session or program and you feel that it does not mean anything to you, then it will not mean anything to God. Your intentions in any fasting and prayer session, is what matters to God. The Scriptures have also cautioned us about going to the public or market place to broadcast it when we fast. When you fast and keep it to yourself, your Heavenly Father, who is omnipresent and omniscience, and who sees in secret, will see and hear you, and will reward you publicly.

When you fast and pray do so in faith and believe that God answers prayers. As the Bible tells us in James 5:16: "The effectual fervent prayer of a righteous man avails much". Do not attempt to block the answer to your prayers by thinking that because you are a sinner or worse still, that you are the worst sinner and therefore that God will not listen to you, and answer your prayers. If you are one of those who always think that they are so terrible and unfit or unworthy to pray to God, read what the Bible teaches us in Romans 3:23, which says that *"All have sinned, and come short of the glory of God"*. All we like sheep have gone astray and the Scripture says in 1 John 1:8-9 that *"If we say that we have no sin, we deceive ourselves and the truth is not in us."* But *"If we confess our sins, God is faithful and just to forgive us and to cleanse us from all unrighteousness"*.

Also, in Romans 10:13, the Bible says that, *"For whosoever shall call upon the name of the Lord shall be saved"*. In Revelation 21:6B-7, God said *"I will give of the fountain of the water of life freely to him who thirsts. He who overcomes shall inherit all things, and I will be his God and he shall be my son"*. We must therefore not relent, but remain steadfast in our daily relationship with God, knowing that there is a crown waiting for us at the end of the race, and because those that endure to the end shall inherit the earth as the Scripture tells us.

In our daily walk with the Lord, we need to ask Him to teach us more and more each day, so we may be better prepared and ready to serve and worship Him as long as we live. Let us not forget that God is a rewarder of those that diligently seek Him, and we must do so while we still have breath. Indeed, each and every one of us has a destiny gene inside of us and those genes represent our divine calling or mission, and we must, therefore, not let them die in us. There is a song that tends to give us a wise advice on our spiritual journey and it goes as follows:

> **It's not an easy road**
> **We are travelling to Heaven**
> **For many are the thorns on the way**
> **It's not an easy load**
> **But the Savior is with us**

Indeed, to follow Jesus, who is the way, the truth, and the life, is not an easy road to walk. But if we commit everything we have to the fame and glory of Jesus, we will be marveled as to what He can do to our lives, and as we honor Him. Remember that Jesus did not negotiate glory. Rather, glory was bestowed on Him. As King David said, I will rather be a doorkeeper in God's House than to be a prince in the tents of wickedness, and also as Joshua said (Joshua 24:15): *"Choose ye this day whom ye will serve......; but as for me and my house, we will serve the Lord"*. You need to make your own decision today. The race to Heaven is a personal one; we cannot delegate it.

Jesus said in Revelation 3:20, *"Behold I stand at the door, and knock; if any man hear My voice, and open the door, I will come in to him, and I will sup with him, and he with Me"*. Irrespective of this Scripture, we sometimes see situations where the Master (Jesus) is knocking on the door of His own Church but the Church do not hear Him knocking, because we are not walking in the Spirit. Hear the Master today, as He knocks on the door of your heart and let Him in into your life. Do not continue to procrastinate and delay your salvation, for tomorrow may be too late.

Have you ever faced any challenges in your life, or have you ever seen trials and tribulations in your life? If so, then you are not alone but on the same boat with many other believers, which calls for improving your attitude and increasing your time towards fasting, prayer, devotion, and dedication to the work of God. When trials and tribulations seem to overwhelm you, it is time to intensify your fasting and prayer life. It is the time to lift up your eyes to the hills from whence cometh my help; it is the time to get closer and develop a more intimate relationship with God.

Let's not give the enemy any room to encroach into our lives, for when you give him an inch, he takes a mile. Remember the servant of God, named Job, in the Old Testament Scriptures and his infamous life story. If this servant of God was able to declare, at the end of the extreme trials and tribulations he endured in a very short period of his life, and say *"I know my Redeemer Liveth"*, then no one of us can actually give up on God to be in the enemy's camp.

Always let the devil know that you are souled out completely to God and therefore, that there is no room and no vacancy for him in your life. Hence, you are all filled up with the power of the Holy Ghost and that Christ who is our hoe of glory, now lives in you.

Let's not give the enemy any room to encroach into our lives, for when you give him an inch, he takes a mile.

Rather, let's always put on the whole armor of God; for the weapons of our warfare are not carnal; they are rather spiritual and mighty to the pulling down of strong holds. This then means that we must fast and pray without ceasing. For a Christian to live day-by-day without prayers is synonymous to a soldier who is sent to the battle field without a weapon. He/she will definitely become an easy prey to the enemy, and you do not want to see yourself in such situation. You don't want to be labeled "Missing in Action" (MIA), do you?

A Closing Prayer

Now that you have finished reading this Kingdom message, if you truly know down in your heart that you are either an unbeliever or a believer but you find yourself still "wearing a mask" and practicing the ungodly things you have previously renounced when you first gave your life to Christ, then humbly say the following short prayer in your heart. (While you're praying, remember that Jesus said that He did not come for the righteous but for sinners to repentance; and in Luke 15:4 He tells us as follows: *"I say unto you, that likewise joy shall be in heaven over one sinner that repenteth, more than over ninety and nine just persons, which need no repentance".*) You may now begin to pray as follows:

My Heavenly Father and my Creator, I know that I have sinned against you, and I regret of the things I have done. Please forgive me for disobeying your Commandments. I will trust and obey you and particularly, I will love you with all my heart, with all my strength, and with all my soul. Cleanse and purify me, and make me what you want me to be. I love you Lord, and I will henceforth live according to your words and do as Mary Magdalene did after you saved her from the mob of Pharisees and then instructed her to "Go, and sin no more". Father, in the name of Jesus, I pray that you grant me the serenity to accept the

> *things I cannot change, the courage to change the things I am able to, and the wisdom to differentiate between them. Thank you, my Father, for hearing my prayer, in Jesus name. Amen.*

It is done, and it is well with you. Go and practice what you have read, and never forget to always go along with the Sword of the Spirit, which is the Word of God, in all your journeys. Don't be fooled, and believe it or not, Heaven and hell are real and it's your choice to decide which route you want to take; there is no "go in between" in this particular case. An old Christian song says: Your hands are worshipping God, your legs are worshipping idols, and your heart is wondering in the world, which side are you? Whose report do you believe? Beloveth, know that just as no two objects can occupy the same space, no one can serve two masters and remain faithful to both of them. Come to Jesus today and accept Him as your Lord and Savior, for tomorrow may be too late, and no one knows tomorrow.

Grace and Peace of our Lord and Savior, Jesus Christ, rest and abide with you now and forevermore. Amen. Shalom!

END NOTES

Unless otherwise stated, all Scripture quotations are from The Thompson Chain-Reference Bible, Fifth Improved Edition, compiled and edited by Frank Charles Thompson, D.D., Ph.D., Copyright 1988 by B.B. Kirkbride Bible Company, Indianapolis, Indiana, USA.

1. The term "True Discipleship" or "True Believer" is synonymous to the word 'Christocracy', meaning the governance of Jesus on earth by His people, or the governance of Jesus Christ on earth through His people, which was originated and defined by His Grace, Archbishop Dr. Joseph A. Alexander, the General Overseer & the Presiding Prelate of the New Covenant Christian Ministries, Worldwide (NCCMW), a global assembly of Churches, Christian Schools, College of Ministries, and a Dominion Wealth Foundation. The word 'Christocracy', which is not yet listed in any dictionary or in any portion of the Bible, was first used by the Archbishop in the year of Our Lord 2011.

2. In the Federal Republic of Nigeria, there is a very powerful anti-malaria medicine called "Daraprim" which is nicknamed "The Sunday, Sunday Medicine". This medicine's nickname became the popular name used in that nation to describe those group of Christians, or better still, "Church-goers" who attend the Church services on Sundays only and then, maybe, on Christmas Day, Easter and New Year's Eve, but live unworthy and worldly lives for the rest six days of the week every year.

ABOUT THE AUTHOR

Clifford N. Opurum, Ph.D., MCIT, is a servant of God, and a True Believer. He is a seasoned Professor of Transportation/Aviation & Logistics, Management, Economics and Business Administration, an accomplished Author, and an Ordained Deacon, and has served in the Office of the Deaconate Ministry for more than seventeen years. He is also a Chorister, and has been a member of the New Covenant Dominion Choir Ministry since 2005. Deacon Dr. Opurum is the General Secretary of the New Covenant Dominion Kingdom Men's Fellowship, and he is also one of the officers of the Church Finance Committee. He is currently serving on the Board of Directors of the New Covenant Dominion Federal Credit Union (NCDFCU), where he previously served as the Chairman of its Credit Committee, and briefly as the Treasurer.

Deacon Dr. Opurum holds a Ph.D. from the University of Leeds, England (2005), three Master's Degrees, respectively, from the State University of New York Maritime College (1985), Fordham University (1987), and the Polytechnic University (1994). He earned his Undergraduate degree from the University of London, England in 1982, and he is currently enrolled in the Ambassadors College of Ministry, where he has taken some courses in the areas of Biblical Counseling & Practice, and Philosophy of Christian Education.

From 1988 to 1991, he served on the New York City Senior Citizens Transportation Advisory Committee and concurrently as a member of the New York City Transportation Task Force during the administrations of Mayors Edward I. Koch and David N. Dinkins. During that same period, he worked for the City of New York as a Community Coordinator and Program Officer (Contract Manager), and also played an active role in the planning, design and implementation of the City's premier para-transit program – the Access-A-Ride. From 1991 to 1994, he served as the Regional Manager for the New York/New Jersey/Connecticut (Tri-State) Region's Transportation and Demographics Activities Monitoring Program at the New York Metropolitan Transportation Council of the New York State Department of Transportation. Also, from 1997 to 2004, he served as a Planner in the Operations Planning Department of New York Metropolitan Transportation Authority's Metro-North Railroad. He presently teaches for The City University of New York and in the School of Architecture at Pratt Institute.

Deacon Dr. Opurum is married, and resides in New York with his dearly beloved wife and children who he refers to as his Blessing, and Precious Promises of God. Prior to their present home Church, the New Covenant Christian Ministries, Deacon Dr. Opurum and his wife attended the Church of the Revelation in the Soundview section of The Bronx, New York, where they were joined together in Holy Matrimony. They met each other at the Times Square Church in Manhattan, New York City, New York.

OTHER BOOKS BY THE AUTHOR

Other books/publications by Deacon Dr. Opurum include:

❖ *Automated Fare Collection System & Urban Public Transportation: An Economic and Management Approach to Urban Transit Systems, Trafford Publishing Company, U.S.A., 2012. (An award-winning book.)*

❖ *Globalization & Regional Integration: The ECOWAS Model, (featured as Chapter 16 of Globalization of Business: Theories and Strategies for Tomorrow's Managers, Adonis & Abbey Publishers Ltd, London, 2008.*

Some of his books are featured on his websites at www.cliffordopurum.authorsxpress.com and www. mytransitbook.com.